WHEN ALL THE WORLD WAS YOUNG

EDNA MacCUISH (née LEATHER) was born and educated in Bolton, Lancashire. She trained and worked as a radiographer at Bolton Royal Infirmary before marrying and moving to Yorkshire. Her three grown-up children having left home Edna studied as a mature student at Bradford University and took a B.Sc. (Hons) degree in 1976. Since then she has taught English Language and Literature at 'O' and 'A' levels at Shipley College and Fox's School of Commerce in Bradford and was an examiner, for a number of years, in English for the Royal Society of Arts and also an Inspector for the R.S.A. Over the years she has had articles, poetry, children's and magazine stories published. As a member of the Lancashire Authors' Association she has been successful several times in the annual competitions mainly in the prose and poetry sections; having once won the play section she has ambitions to become a playwright. Although still living in Yorkshire, Edna is a thorough Lancastrian at heart.

When all the world was young

A Bolton childhood in the thirties

by

Edna MacCuish

♦JADE♦

Jade Publishing Limited,
5, Leefields Close, Uppermill, Oldham, Lancashire, OL3 6LA.

This first edition published by Jade Publishing Limited 1993.

ISBN 0 9518098 3 0 When all the world was young. (Pbk).

Printed in Great Britain by
Browns Colour Printers Limited, Oldham, Lancashire.

Typeset in Plantin by
Jade Publishing Limited, Uppermill, Oldham, Lancashire.

A CIP catalogue record for this book is available
from the British Library

For Allison, David and Fiona

Acknowledgements

The author's grateful thanks are due to many relatives and friends for encouragement, supplementary memories and the loan of photographs.

The author is also deeply appreciative of the help she received from Eric Holt who so willingly wrote the Foreword; Nell Ashcroft who set the book on the road to publication; Brian Prescott who undertook to publish; Noëlle Vickers for editing the book and Margaret McClay who worked so tirelessly and cheerfully to prepare the MS.

Contents

Photographs

Foreword

by Eric Holt

In "She Stoops to Conquer" by Oliver Goldsmith there is a speech, "I love everything that's old: old friends, old times, old manners, old books, old wine." To this can be added, 'old tales', for these are the very essence of our memories. When reminiscing and sifting through the tumbled oddments of the past, it is usually some particular tale which triggers off an explosion of anecdotes.

These thoughts came to mind when I was asked to write this foreword. I must admit that, although I know the writer of this book, I did not know the characters she so lovingly portrays. But I did know of the time, and I certainly know the place — Bolton. Pre-1939 was a special period for me, being the last years of an epoch which was never to be seen again. The war saw to that. Changes came about which had a traumatic effect on all our futures.

Edna MacCuish, in this book, has turned a keen eye and a perceptive mind on pre-war Bolton. Her people are very recognisable people. They are the ordinary folk of an essentially typical Northern industrial town. Added to this keen eye is a retentive memory, and an accomplished writer's way with words. In this respect I can truly give unstinting praise. From my work with the Lancashire Authors' Association I know Edna to be a writer of delightful poems, imaginative, observant, and never less than beautifully constructed.

This art she brings to her prose writings. By the happy choice of a word, and the apt turn of a phrase the common-place can become magical. Edna MacCuish, obviously, loves her memories just as she loves the people who made these memories. And now she shares them with us, bringing a taste of how Bolton was before the war.

If you are old enough — remember, and enjoy. If not — just enjoy!

Eric Holt
Westhoughton
Bolton
August, 1993

Preface

'From quiet homes and first beginning,
Out to the undiscovered ends,
There's nothing worth the wear of winning,
But laughter and the love of friends.'

Hilaire Belloc — Dedicatory Ode

There is an indestructible magic about unforgettable days. We never escape our beginnings nor should we. Many days in our lives mingle with others until, like coins worn by constant circulation, their image and superscription are completely obliterated. They disappear from memory as though they had never been. Fortunately others remain fresh, distinct and rich in detail as though newly-minted.

Memory can only refer to itself, can only in a sense remember itself. It cannot restore but it can, imperfectly, re-create the past.

CHAPTER 1

First Beginning

No trams ran in Bolton on Sunday mornings during the 1920s. The whole town fell into a state of suspended animation. Workers had the day off and factory hooters stayed silent. Nothing more than the rattle of milk floats broke the morning quiet. Most people were either housebound or churchbound.

"What's done on Sunday comes undone on Monday," mother would say as she consigned any ongoing bits of knitting or sewing to the sideboard drawer for the day. And off we went to church. After dinner, my brother Gordon and I set off again, bound for Sunday School. When we emerged at three o'clock there were signs of life and movement on the streets, albeit sedate, and for us it was the turning point of the day.Our parents, more often than not, took us out. To justify this pleasurable act of Sabbath breaking, my mother selected another quote: "The better the day the better the deed." For years I imagined our visits to family and friends on Sundays could be interpreted as missions of mercy.

1

One sunny Sunday afternoon, I remember, mother wore her flowered crêpe de chine dress to complement the intense and unexpected heat. Her accessories, brown straw cloche hat, brown handbag and shoes, and rope of amber beads added the finishing touches, together with a muscavado-brown summer coat, in case a cool breeze suddenly sprang up. Susceptible to the vagaries of Lancashire weather, mother rarely ventured far without a coat. And never on Sunday. As a final gesture to fashion and propriety, cream cotton gloves completed the outfit.

Beside her, my father looked uncomfortably hot and formal in his best navy blue suit, waistcoat, stiff winged collar and bowler hat. He might have dispensed with his waistcoat but then, where would he have kept his gold pocket watch with its chain traversing his middle? His black Sunday shoes squeaked when he walked. Gordon, with all the bravado of a seven-year old, remarked that the squeak meant the shoes had not been paid for. My father, not amused, silenced him with "That will do" as we prepared to set off, that rare and glorious June Sunday, to visit the Wrays at Farnworth.

Gordon and I also sported our Sunday clothes. Anything less than the best and we should have considered ourselves, and been considered by neighbours and friends, as deviants. We proudly conformed to the image of respectability.

Sunday outings were the high point of the week. My father was at home all day. Immediately after breakfast we would ask, "Where are we going today?" If the answer was "Nowhere" then we changed it to "Who's coming to tea?" Sunday, in Lancashire, was a day for either visiting or being visited, especially for tea.

The prospect of Mrs. Wray's tea cheered us. We anticipated the tinned salmon and salad, tinned peaches with Carnation milk and Russian sandwich cake correctly. This was standard fare although boiled ham supplanted salmon

2

sometimes on high days and holidays. After tea the adults decided a stroll along the streets of Farnworth would neatly round off the day: though the children were less than enthusiastic about the walk, open rebellion was unthinkable. I offered to trundle young Madge Wray in her pushchair, while Gordon and the Wray twins, Joan and Jean, ran on ahead.

Before long, I noticed Gordon and the twins hopping from one paving stone to the next, avoiding the cracks. It was an exciting game and they called to me to join in. At first, I spurned the invitation. Yet hearing the shouts of laughter and seeing them revelling in the fun of hopping and jumping, I began to feel dissatisfied with my lot. Suddenly they started chanting:

'Tread on a nick and you'll marry a stick
And a beetle will come to your wedding!'

That did it. I was seized with unrestrained envy. Walking sedately along behind the rattling old Tan-Sad seemed a wearisome chore. On an impulse I threw caution to the warm June air and set off to join in the fun, careless of the consequences. And Madge, sitting with her back to me, solid as a suet dumpling, never uttered a murmur of dissent.

With the imprudence of a fun-loving five-year old, I quickened my pace, gripping the pushchair handle like a drowning man clutching a straw. Soon a noticeable difference in the rhythm of the pram wheels sparked a warning in my mind as I broke into a run. We gathered speed, the pushchair, Madge and I, on the slight downhill gradient of the street. In a matter of moments the situation got out of hand. I lost control. To halt the accelerating, crazily careering pram became impossible. I tried to scream but no sound came out.

The adults who, up to now, had seemed becalmed by deep and earnest conversation realised what was happening and were spurred into action.

3

"Stop! For goodness sake stop!" My mother's terrified voice dimly reached my panic-stricken mind. But it was too late. The pushchair with my fingers clamped round the handle in a paralysis of desperation, plunged wildly along, targeted on a cast iron lamp-post. My feet flew over the pavement as the pram bore me along in a haze of speed. Despite the perpetual motion I was dimly aware of doors flung open at intervals, and anxious faces peering out but no one attempted to prevent the inevitable.

The resulting encounter of the pushchair with the gas lamp created an explosion of metallic sound. Then there was silence until Madges's shrieks of fright, and my mother's cries of horror, shattered it. I stood, dumb with shame and abject terror, my fingers welded to that pushchair handle. I felt a stinging slap on my leg. Astonishment superceded tears at first. Looking up I watched my mother's face turn from bright red to parchment white as anger and amazement contended for dominance. Physical punishment was something I had previously never experienced. The slap came as a tremendous shock. But then the hubbub of noise all round me, Madge's incessant crying, the distraught look on mother's face opened the floodgates. Tears flowed like a steady downpour.

"Well, what's come over you, I don't know" mother declared, stuffing her gloves in her handbag. "She deserves a good hiding," my father put in without being prepared to carry it out. Mother prised my deadened fingers from the pram handle, rubbing them back to life. "You could have killed Madge if she hadn't been strapped in," she added for good measure.

I stayed silent, utterly mortified. Yet, I sensed the white heat of my mother's anger was waning for her tone had become more reproachful than bitter, and she started to pull on her gloves again.

Mrs. Wray, robustly practical and cast in the heroic mould, extricated the bawling Madge from the buckled pushchair, before prodding sensitive areas for signs of injury.

4

Everything appeared to be intact and in good working order, especially her lungs. Mrs. Wray's relief fed her irritation and she rounded on the screaming child. "For heaven's sake, shut up, Madge. There's nothing wrong with you." Incredibly, Madge obliged. The sudden absence of sound had the effect of a ceasefire. Everyone relaxed.

Next, Mrs. Wray turned her attention to me, begging me to, "Buck up, love and dry your eyes. It's not a catastrophe."

"I'm sorry, Mrs. Wray. I didn't mean it," I said tearfully, after being prompted to apologise by a cuff on the shoulder from my mother.

"Don't fret yourself. All's well as ends well I say," Mrs. Wray laughed. She was a good-hearted woman, understanding and completely without rancour. As far as she was concerned the unfortunate mishap was dismissed, finished. I smiled tremulously, in gratitude. It was then I began to search my dress pockets, puff sleeves, knicker legs — all in vain.

"Where's your clean hanky?" mother said coldly.

"I haven't got one!"

"No clean hanky!" In mother's eyes this amounted to a cardinal sin. Almost worse than crashing the pushchair. She paused. In the face of this extra disaster her composure was admirable. "Well." She always began with 'Well' in time of stress. "I'll lend you mine for this once." Having a clean handkerchief was, according to my mother, next to godliness.

The rest of the evening was ruined of course. Drying my eyes I joined the subdued little group trooping back to Moses Gate to catch the tram home.

My father, always at his finest in a crisis, doled out compensation for the distress I had caused. The twins received a three-penny bit each and Madge a whole silver sixpence as a reward for having so narrowly avoided death. Mother hesitated on the tram step to make a further apology.

Mrs. Wray, with characteristic exuberance called "Now don't bother your head about it, Maggie, there's no harm done. Sorry you're off so soon."

The tram started to move. "Ta-ra", the Wrays called blithely, waving frantically as though we were emigrating on the *Queen Mary* rather than travelling a few miles on a tram.

Only Gordon, as brothers do, extracted excitement and drama out of the incident. He pondered on it all the way from Moses Gate to Trinity Street, for, as we changed trams and boarded one for Tonge Moor, he whispered in my ear: "You were nearly a murderer. Did you know that?" And, to re-inforce this grisly piece of information, he aimed a half-hearted kick at my shins with his black Sunday boot, demonstrating his delight at the prospect of regaling his pals with the afternoon's events. The tears flowed anew. I knuckled my eyes dry and kept my gaze fixed on the toes of my black patent shoes as the tram clattered and swayed its way up the broo to the Starkie.

By the time we reached home I sensed a warmer atmosphere prevailing. The next morning I knew for certain all was forgiven.

Nevertheless, my mother, still upset by the incident, took me back to the Wrays two days later, bearing a newly baked loaf as a peace-offering. She reassured herself Madge was none the worse for her ordeal, made me apologise once more, and presented the loaf to Mrs. Wray.

After this my mother never referred to the incident again. Neither did we see much of the Wrays.

We lived at this time at number 17 George Barton Street, in the Tonge Moor district of Bolton, where the terraced cottages stood like a string of paper cut-outs all

Edna's mother, Margaret, when about forty years old.

Edna's father, Arthur Leather, in his late thirties.

Grandpa Allinson.

Edna, aged five, and brother Gordon, seven, in 1931.

At a church bazaar mock-wedding in 1930. (*Left*) Gordon Leather, aged six, as the smart bridegroom to the smiling bride, Barbara Rushton, aged four. (*Right*) Attentive bridesmaid Edna, aged four, clutching her bouquet tightly with a commanding Jack Davis as best man.

exactly the same, two up two down, front doors opening on to the pavement, modest back yards giving access to the back street. Net curtains covered the windows like eyelids.

George Barton Street was one of three streets forming a triangle, separated by an island of cinders surrounded by pavement. These three streets formed part of a wider area of housing which had been built totally ad hoc for the mill workers and miners of the district of Tonge Moor.

Then, as now, they were much sought after by first-time buyers. Number 17 became my parents' first home. Gordon and I were born there. Our house boasted electricity, a porcelain kitchen sink and a lavatory in the backyard which flushed. Luxuries my grandparents never experienced. Its restricted size added to its cosiness.

In our street, windows gleamed, front steps were scrubbed white and donkey stoned; a credit to the constant vigilance of the women folk who waged a relentless battle against grime and soot. From every chimney, smoke plumed seven days a week for ten or eleven months of the year. Smoke belched too from mill chimneys six days a week. A canopy of grey, gritty haze hung over Bolton. We walked beneath it unperturbed by its potential threat to health. Our parents accepted it philosophically knowing they were impotent to change it and we learnt early the streets were paved, not with gold, but with tough, hard cobblestones. Our world revolved round industry.

My mother's skirmishes with soot and grime made her stoical. She accepted them as part of the eternal plan of our existence. They could never be eradicated. "We've all to eat a peck of dirt in our lifetime", she said in one of her more placid moods.

Although my parents, particularly my mother, spoke yearningly of the countryside, they knew it remained almost out of bounds most of the time. And their knowledge of country matters was minimal, an oak or an elm was all the same to them. Their wisdom and expertise encompassed town living. My father, a dark-haired, dark-eyed man, compact and strong, was intensely practical, he could make and mend most things around the house. He left home very early each morning, lighting the fire before setting out for work at Haslam's sheet metal works in Randall Street, off Bury Road. The fire never failed to 'catch' at the first match. Often he used no more than four paper chips, expertly created from the Bolton Evening News, and a few pieces of coal. He scorned both wood and firelighters. Only rarely was my mother obliged to lay and light the fire and in her less experienced hands it smouldered sulkily for long enough until, in a fit of frustration, she threw the contents of the sugar bowl on it. The fire responded with a blaze and a blast which sent us reeling to the middle door.

My mother's talents thrived in home-making pursuits. Her home and family constituted her life and we, as children, benefitted from the pleasure and satisfaction she derived from creating a home that was comfortable, secure and happy. In return we never doubted the rightness of our parents' code of conduct.

Though sparsely furnished, our home was warm and welcoming. Gordon and I were happy to be nurtured on the staff of life and a set of imperishable maxims applicable to each and every situation we encountered.

'Children should be seen and not heard' became a byword in the family, so did 'Speak only when you are spoken to' and 'Never answer back your elders and betters.' Our minor surges of intransigence were quelled by firm words and stern looks from my father. We learnt from an early age that mother was a soft option but on matters of behaviour father set the boundaries beyond which we ventured at our peril.

As children, our parents had been weighed down by the stultifying baggage of Victorian moral values which only gradually eroded in the slowly expanding social scene of the 1930s. Some were maintained in our childhood. Regular attendance at church and Sunday School, for instance. We discarded these, initially, with guilt. Still, our behaviour was controlled by our parents' invocation of certain moral categories of good and bad, right and wrong and responsibility and respect for our elders. This moral basis held firm during our formative years. It bred in us, as it had in them, a taste for independence and respect for personal privacy. We recoiled at rushing in where angels feared to tread. On the negative side, however, we developed a host of inhibitions, which took us decades to come to terms with, let alone displace.

Our first beginning, compared with that of our parents, was immensely privileged and the influence on Gordon and me of my mother's side of the family remains incalculable.

CHAPTER 2

The Allinsons

Before the twentieth century was a decade old, seven Allinson children left number 30 Lenora Street, Deane, six mornings a week bound for the mill or school. Their parents John and Mary Ellen nurtured this brood of three sons and four daughters in the small terrace house with amazing proficiency considering their straitened circumstances and cramped conditions.

My mother, Margaret, the fifth child and third daughter, had the unfortunate distinction of being the weakest member of the family. Even so, the rigours of the hard life were inescapable. The implacable economic conditions demanded that everyone became a wage-earner at the earliest opportunity and by 12 years of age she began working as a half-timer, mornings at school, afternoons at the mill, joining the army of clog-shod workers looking after two looms.

John, mother's youngest brother, stationed himself at the back gate each morning, calling out rousing remarks to any stragglers. As mother came tumbling out of the house, buttoning her coat and clutching her sandwiches, John cried cheerily, 'Mind you don't turn sideways, Maggie, otherwise you'll disappear.' And mother, thin to the point of skinniness, endured his teasing with a smile, though it stung.

Grandma Allinson, worn out with childbearing and seldom free from the pain of arthritis, devised a housekeeping rota for her four daughters which became operational whenever she felt ill. The girls took it in turns to stay at home from school in the mornings and cope with the chores. To have missed the afternoon shift at the mill would have been reprehensible, earning no wages. Morning school proved the easy sacrifice. My mother's absences from school increased as grandma's health deteriorated and her older sisters, Emily and Lizzie, became employed full-time. Although bitterly regretting her lack of education in later life, mother conceded this early training in housewifery prepared her well for marriage.

The Allinsons, an uncomplicated and predictable family, slipped into the mainstream of Bolton life with the gentlest of ripples. They were certainly never ones to make a splash. Yet within the circumscribed limits of their family and social circle, their lives were enriched by much laughter and the loving affection of friends.

During hard times, appetites were regulated by the position in the family hierarchy. At breakfast, grandpa and grandma had a whole egg, the eldest four children, Fred, Emily, Herbert and Elizabeth merited half an egg, the next two, Margaret and John, shared the tops of their parents' eggs, while Ellen, the youngest, had to be satisfied with fingers of bread dipped in the yolk of her mother's egg. Such economies were submitted to without complaint. Any grumbles brought a sharp rebuke from grandpa, who pursued a consistent policy of 'get on with life and no grousing'.

In appearance Grandpa Allinson was portly with a face of fresh complexion and a pre-occupied expression making him appear grave. His silver hair, moustache and spectacles accentuated this air of seriousness which belied his

12

underlying kindliness. His sober suits of clerical grey or black reflected the serious side of his nature exactly. Only on Saturdays did he allow himself the indulgence of removing his stiff white collar for an hour at tea-time and loosening the collar stud of his union shirt. Within his own family he remained an authoritarian figure. But to his grandchildren he was invariably genial and benevolent.

According to my mother, he invented cellular material but, unprotected by a patent, allowed his discovery to slip into the hands of his employers, who reaped the rewards. His working life was spent as manager of Deane Weaving Shed. He never shirked his duties nor expected his children to do so. They accepted that being immured in the mill 12 hours a day, six days a week, was an unalterable fact of life and endured it with cheerful fortitude. Only Herbert rebelled, yet he had to comply until the First World War rescued him from the drudgery of a job for which he was neither physically nor mentally equipped.

Heavy furniture and bitter-chocolate brown paint over-burdened the Allinson home and it always took several moments to register my bearings when I wandered in from the street. Objects merged in the gloom, but once I located the aspidistra in its bottle green pot and the two lustre jugs on either side of it, I made my way over the brown linoleum to the rag rug in front of the great black iron range, where the fire glowed dimly and continuously beneath a bank of slack, and grandma, swathed from head to foot in black serge overtopped with a sombre grey shawl, rocked rhythmically and contentedly in her chair. In repose, her face had the delicate fragility and refinement of a Victorian china doll.

The living room was redolent of spicy pickles and cheeses, housed in the enormous sideboard. Grandpa possessed a discerning palate. While the rest of the family ate mousetrap Cheddar, he indulged his passion for Gorgonzola. A good chunk of Lancashire cheese provided a rich treat on Saturdays and everyone enjoyed a pickled onion with their cheese by his kind permission.

13

Hanging on the wall beside the sideboard, a well-stocked smoking cabinet held a variety of pipes, cleaners, matches and tobacco. Grandpa's special favourite was an intriguingly shaped Meerschaum. He had a passion for it. Yet he denied himself the pleasure of smoking until the clearing of the tea-table was complete. Then he would take out his gold Hunter watch, flip open the cover and check the time with that of the pendulum clock. When they synchronised at six o'clock precisely, he deftly tucked the watch back in his waistcoat pocket and lifted the Meerschaum from the smoking cabinet. The moment the pipe was well alight was the one grandpa savoured above all others, the Meerschaum moment.

Despite its austere dimness, the house held a tangible atmosphere of warmth and comfort. The family gravitated to it like filings to a magnet. My mother and her sisters loved it as 'home' even when they had their own houses and families.

On our visits, grandma Allinson with her mild brown eyes and slow smile, listened to my childish prattle without interruption until I ran out of breath. She was the perfect audience. Then she produced two tins from a shelf beside her and offered me a choice of Uncle Joe's mintballs or striped humbugs. Grandpa Allinson deplored verbosity and, when the recital ended, would invite me to sit quietly on the horsehair sofa while I sucked my sweet offering me a choice of Punch or The Tatler as reading matter. For a short time, silence reigned. Only the pendulum clock with its regular tick intruded.

It was not long though before one or two horsehairs, sprouting through the black, shiny covering of the couch began to tickle my legs. I felt compelled to scratch, and the magazines slithered to the floor, closely followed by me. Swivelling his head round from his seat at the table, grandpa peered over the top of his steel rimmed specs with a wounded expression and scratched his head. Squirming with nervousness, I'd say, 'I'll go and find my mother and see if Aunty Nellie and Winifred have come.'

14

Mother was inevitably in the kitchen. Aunty Nellie and Winifred came as support and sometimes Aunty Lizzie. Mother and her sisters chattered incessantly when they met at Lenora Street, but confined their conversation and laughter to the kitchen. They respected their father's desire for silence in the house and in his presence were restrained. Winifred and I played outdoors whenever possible and spoke in whispers if we stayed in.

After tea grandpa, smoking his Meerschaum, filled the room with clouds of smoke which gathered about the gas mantles, dimming their pale yellow domes and restricting our view of each other. But once the first pipe of the evening was finished he rose from the table, fished two sixpences from his top waistcoat pocket and handed them to Winifred and me. Then he replaced his winged collar, buttoned himself into his jacket and overcoat, settled his bowler hat in place and sallied forth to the Junction hostelry where, with a lifelong commitment to inaccessibility as far as the family was concerned, he spent Saturday evenings in quiet conversation with his cronies until closing time.

Hardly had the front door closed behind him before mother and Aunty Nellie, Aunty Lizzie having been driven off to the first house at the Grand Theatre by Uncle Arnold, began an animated and uninterrupted conversation. Grandma poked the fire into life, sparks flew and flames leapt up the chimney-back in joyous celebration of release. The kettle snorted and spat on the hob. More tea was brewed. Suddenly the room was lighter, cosier. Laughter bubbled from us. Even grandma chuckled appreciatively as she listened to her daughters' light-hearted banter. Their presence comforted her. Winifred and I squatted on the rag rug deciding how best to spend our silver sixpences, which we had received from grandfather with pleasure and gratitude.

After the excitement and extra liquid refreshment, mother deemed a journey to the 'tippler' essential before our departure home. She always accompanied me to this

15

chamber of horrors. The apparently bottomless black shaft, the gurgling of flowing water and the wooden seat with a hole on which I perched in terror clinging to my mother, paralysed me. To my fevered imagination this mineshaft might easily suck me into its depths if I so much as wobbled. My bladder refused to function.

"Have you finished?" Mother soon grew impatient.

"I've not started yet."

"Listen to the water then."

"I am listening."

"Well, then?"

"I can't go." In the end mother hauled me off the seat in exasperation, bundled me back into the house, threw on my outdoor clothes and her own with such unseemly haste, Grandma was prompted to remark,

"Maggie, all this rushing gives me palpitations."

But undeterred, mother made a speedy departure, anxious to get me home before an 'accident' occurred. Aunty Nellie was left to soothe Grandma, with the aid of a dash of brandy, back to her habitual state of rocking contentment.

Number 30 Lenora Street was a quiet, serious house. One to grow wise in if you had a leaning for reading and meditation. Laughter echoed there mainly in Grandpa Allinson's absence. I often wonder if he had any inkling of the damper his presence created, for he was kind and generous to us children. But to his own brood he was a man to be feared rather than loved. The only time the tranquility of the house was shattered by screams, they happened to be mine.

By some immutable family agreement winter Saturdays belonged to my Allinson grandparents. Immediately after our mid-day dinner, mother dressed me ready for the journey to Deane. My father and Gordon sometimes arrived at Lenora Street at tea-time to accompany us home, other times they visited our paternal grandparents.

One winter Saturday mother and I arrived at Grandma Allinsons as usual in the afternoon. The previous day snow had fallen which thawed overnight, turning into grey slippery slush. Although I wore my wellingtons, I somehow contrived to get them wet inside. So when we arrived at Lenora Street, mother pulled them off and stuffed them with newspaper, setting them by the range to dry.

Winifred and I played indoors all afternoon, communicating in whispers and stifling our laughter. Grandpa, pleased to have been left more or less undisturbed, remarked that our sixpences were well-earned. We glowed with pleasure. After he departed for his evening of bibulous conviviality at the Junction, mother suggested we might like to spend one penny of our sixpences at the corner shop, as a special treat for our good behaviour. We did not need a second bidding.

But when I came to put on my wellingtons, mother discovered they were still damp inside.

"Let her wear mine," Aunty Nellie said generously. She laughed. "They're about five sizes too big, but it is only two minutes to the shop. You'll be able to paddle there and back."

My thin legs sprouting from the top of these wide wellingtons provided a source of amusement to everyone except me.

Across from the house a patch of uneven spare land held a cluster of huts on the far side and we had to cross this on our way to the shop. Progress was slow as my feet slipped backwards, forwards and sideways inside the wellingtons like loose cargo in a ship's hold. Clinging to Winifred, I eventually negotiated the slush-covered mounds and hollows and we reached the pavement. It was very dark. Only two faintly flickering gas lamps lit the whole area. Most of the street lay in deep shadow.

We arrived at the shop, agonised over our penny purchases and began our return journey. Winifred opting to run dragged me along behind her as though I were a sledge until we reached the spare ground. Here I was hampered by the flapping wellingtons and Winifred had to slow down. No sooner had we started across the rough slushy land when

17

a man's dark figure loomed from behind one of the sheds. I froze as his hand came down on my arm. "Come with me," he muttered, pulling me away from Winifred.

I screamed. Winifred fled. My scream may have unnerved him because I managed to twist away and jerk my arm free. No longer paralysed with fear I set off after Winifred but before I had taken more than a few strides, the oversized wellingtons skidded on the wet slush and I sprawled flat on the ground. Rigid with terror, I expected to feel the hand grip me again and haul me off. I screamed again and again. Nothing happened so I scrambled to my feet. Fear kept me upright as I ran blindly, heedless of the unwieldy wellingtons, in pursuit of Winifred. I did not look back but kept my eyes fixed on number 30. As I reached the gate still grasping my bag of aniseed balls, the door opened and mother came rushing down the path.

The whole episode had lasted no more than a few terrifying moments but long enough to send me into a state of incoherence. After calming me down, mother and Aunty Nellie went to report the incident to the police. According to them we had escaped lightly.

Aunty Nellie blamed the wellingtons and mother blamed the weather. Though neither of them blamed Winifred or me, there was no word of praise either for Winifred's heroic dash to alert them to my predicament or my acumen in using my scream as an effective deterrent. That rather took the steam out of the whole affair. We made an early return home with my feet firmly fitted into my own, still damp, wellingtons.

My Allinson uncles kept a low profile when I was young. They had all left the nest at Deane by the time we visited Lenora Street regularly.

The eldest, Frederick, remained no more than a name in the family annals. He never came to our house and we never visited him. Eventually I asked why he was always absent from family gatherings. My mother's explanation, brief and evasive, was to the effect that Uncle Fred had married Milly, who was, not to put too fine a point on it, rather 'common' because of her frizzed and henna-ed hair and the fact that she was not averse to going into a pub. Why Uncle Fred chose Milly for his wife was a mystery to my mother. She and Lizzie and Nellie summarily cut him out of their lives and relied on Uncle John, who harboured no such prejudice against Fred, to keep them informed on his health and happiness, but not Milly's. All further questioning from me on the subject met with firm discouragement and my curiosity withered. One day my mother and I met Milly accidentally in Newport Street. While they talked my eyes were riveted to her frizzy and rather brassy-red hair looking like a knitted tea cosy. But she seemed an outgoing, friendly person at that brief encounter. When we parted I wanted to ask all sorts of questions about Milly but mother's expression made silence the better part of prudence. Uncle John described Fred as 'a perfect gentleman, quiet and refined.' I felt deprived of a first rate uncle.

Uncle Herbert, a square peg in a round hole when he slaved at the mill, became a more substantial figure, in fits and starts, during my early years. Tall and thin, he found fulfilment after enlisting in the Royal Artillery in 1914. He was not a born soldier. He did not possess what Napoleon called 'two o'clock in the morning courage.' Yet, undaunted by the rigours of army life and conditions he strove to succeed. His manner, deferential without being obsequious brought him to the notice of his superiors, and his precise way of speaking, combined with exceptional attention to details, gave weight and credence to his declarations on the fortunes of war. He rose swiftly through the ranks and within 18 months found himself promoted to captain. Somewhere along the front line he gathered a Military Medal for a deed of exceptional courage. The family proudly recognised his bravery while simultaneously remembering how, as a child, he fled home from play at the first hint of a fight, fainted at the sight of blood, hid in the cupboard under the stairs whenever his father showed signs of anger and hated getting his boots muddy.

Destiny held a final trick up its sleeve for Herbert. During the last months of fighting in 1918 a young corporal, standing next to him, was shot and fatally wounded. Herbert did what he could but to no avail. Carefully he collected the soldier's personal effects together and was amazed to find the boy hailed from Bolton. His name was Rimmer, the son of the owner of Rimmer's Gents' Outfitters in Bradshawgate. On his return to civvy street Herbert visited the Rimmers, handed over their son's belongings and gave them an account of the tragedy. As a mark of their gratitude Mr. Rimmer offered Herbert a job in his shop. It was the perfect post for him. Promotion to the position of shop manager came in a very short time. His future was secure.

Always a natty dresser with spats, bowler hat, pin-striped suit, with a triangle of white handkerchief tucked smartly into the breast pocket, gloves and furled umbrella, the ambience of a bespoke menswear shop was right up his street.

My acquaintance with Uncle Herbert began when I was five or six years old. He came to us for his midday meal for two or three weeks. Then he disappeared for months on end, only to appear again suddenly for another spell of meals with us. It was during one of these visits I first learned of his musical talent. He arrived one dinner time carrying a long cigar-shaped instrument case along with his furled umbrella. In answer to my mother's queries he removed the instrument from the case, holding it out at arm's length and eyeing it with the fixed expression of a man dedicated to a glorious goal.

"It's an oboe," he said in his precise way.

"Well...," my mother said, all at sea with the unknown. "Well, take your things off, Herbert. Dinner's ready."

20

The oboe was stowed away in its case while we ate our meal. Afterwards my father left for work, Gordon escaped to play in the street and Herbert was left to his own devices while mother busied herself with the washing up and I helped. There was the soft swish of sudsy washing-up water and the clinking sound of dishes piling up on the drainer when, suddenly and unexpectedly, a long, low mournful note boomed into the silence close to mother's ear. Startled, she dropped a Shelley china cup on to the hard composition kitchen floor where it smashed to smithereens. She turned quite pale. The deep sound, sustained for what seemed ages, stopped when Uncle Herbert ran out of breath. His blown out cheeks deflated slowly, his moustache bristled with the continuous pressure on the mouthpiece and his lips took on a wild bilberry hue. He smiled, waiting for a few words of praise and encouragement. He seemed oblivious of the calamity at his feet. Ironically mother only used the best Shelley china when Uncle Herbert came, in deference to his fastidious taste.

"Did that sound all right?" he asked innocently.

My mother replied with some asperity.

"It would've sounded a lot better if you'd bothered to give me some warning, Herbert. Just look at my best Shelley cup. How can I afford another?" She was close to tears. Herbert, looking crestfallen apologised. The oboe returned to its case and he caught an earlier tram than usual back to Bolton.

The next day he arrived with a substitute Shelley cup and minus the oboe. He hoped it was the right size and shape. It wasn't. However, he was forgiven. Soon after he left for work, mother went to town and changed Herbert's breakfast sized replacement for a teacup.

Some six months later, Herbert announced his imminent marriage to a widow, ten years older than himself. Mother sallied forth once more, to Bailey's stall in the covered market and presented the happy couple with a Shelley china tea service.

"Edith will need a few replacements," she confided to me, "if he gives her some unexpected shocks with his oboe."

We did not attend the wedding. It was a quiet affair and Uncle Herbert stayed on the periphery of our lives after his marriage. Edith proved to be a formidable lady with strong features, and a disgruntled expression. Whether they lived happily ever after, no one seems to know.

After Uncle Fred, whose excommunication by his sisters was never rescinded, and Uncle Herbert, an elusive figure in the family circle after pledging his troth to Edith, there remained Uncle John. And he adopted the role of family chronicler, keeping the news circulating. In talent, John was undoubtedly the cleverest of the Allinson brood and the rest of the family acknowledged his authority without question. If his reliability was occasionally dented slightly by a hint of overstatement, he had the ability to overcome this misfortune without flinching, knowing he would never stand corrected by the other members of the family. They held his opinions in awe. Quietly spoken, with a soothing avuncular tone to his voice, he invariably released a reassuring smile when he finished speaking which set everyone nodding and smiling gently in agreement.

Although he resided in Macclesfield from 1926, the year I was born, his ties with Bolton remained strong. He changed his allegiance from cotton to silk and the mills of Cheshire benefitted tremendously from John Allinson's inventive expertise.

Uncle John literally fell into my life one summer afternoon when I was four years old. He had travelled from Macclesfield for the day to visit his parents in Deane, and having some family news to pass on, decided to drop in on us briefly before returning home. Coming through the front door with his usual bouncing step the doormat tripped him up, so he maintained, and he twisted his knee badly. He stayed three days. A telegram conveying the news of this mishap to his family seemed necessary. Aunty Agnes, and

22

their three small daughters might have imagined the worst had he failed to reach home by dusk. The telegram put her mind at rest, but no morbid thoughts had disturbed her anyway. Sensible and level-headed Aunty Agnes sent a nicely worded postcard in reply telling Uncle John to return to Buxton Road as and when he felt able. Until then, life would proceed quite well without him. Aunty Agnes was never one to be ruffled by minor setbacks — or major ones for that matter.

Every do-it-yourself remedy known to my parents was applied to the swollen knee. Bathed and swathed in comfrey leaves, gently massaged withIodex ointment, carefully bound with an elastic bandage and constantly supported by a feather cushion. Mother reckoned John might stay a week she made him so comfortable.

With all the time in the world to spare, Uncle John entertained me with tales of Dickens' characters. Little Nell, Pip and Magwitch, Oliver Twist, Tiny Tim and a host of others. They came as a revelation to me. He adored Dickens, whose novels were his constant companions, and in me he had a captive audience. Story-telling was second nature to him; with three daughters he had no lack of practice.

After dinner on the third day, he limped off to the tram for his journey home. The house seemed suddenly lifeless and empty.

"Shall we go for a nice ta ta," my mother said, "it'll make us feel better."

Ever after that Uncle John stayed with us for no more than a few hours, arriving unexpectedly with his usual bouncing walk. "It's as though he has springs inside him," my mother said, puzzled, being altogether more of a stroller herself. The doormat became a family joke. Sadly the tales from Dickens were never repeated again in such rich and fascinating detail.

Our visits to Macclesfield were few and far between, time and cost being the drawbacks, but the Allinson home on Buxton Road was always open house to anyone wishing to stay. My father took advantage of this ever-available invitation when recuperating from a hernia operation. He stayed for over a week. My mother, waiting daily for a note informing her when he would be home, received the following missive from Uncle John:

Macclesfield
2nd October, 1936

Dear Maggie,

While I refresh myself with a glass of Guinness, your noble husband is sitting on a chair by the fire with his feet up on another perusing the News Chronicle. As it seemed a pity to disturb him, I offered to write to you for him, knowing how anxious you will be to hear news of his progress.

He is now in the best of health, so you need have no worries on that score. We have enjoyed some excellent walks together and have put the world to rights as we ambled through the country lanes. Our mutually beloved and respected Arthur is worth his weight in silk spindles any day.

He will be returning to you the day after to-morrow in tip-top condition. He should arrive in time for tea. We heard from Lizzie yesterday. She says you are in the pink which is so much better than being in the red!

Our love to you all. I expect King Arthur would send his too but, as his head is completely buried in the newspaper, I haven't bothered to ask him about it.

Yours,

John

Such an entertaining and informative letter cheered mother far more than any communication from my father. He would have sent a plain postcard bearing a brief comment regarding the weather followed by the time of his expected arrival home signed with his initial.

If my father was overwhelmed by the Allinson family's talent for producing another relative just when he seemed to have met the lot, he gave no sign of it.

He had but one brother, Thomas, and they were brought up in Halliwell. My father upheld the family tradition of reticence, divulging little of his early life. Both his father and brother were postmen. By apprenticing himself in the sheet metal trade, my father broke the mould.

If the Allinson family home seemed small and gloomy, the Leather's house was dark as a pocket. My grandmother, fat, comfortable and jolly, had a fondness for sentimental pictures and superfluous family paraphernalia. In a carved cedarwood box placed on the high mantleshelf her gallstones were preserved for frequent inspection. They were as precious to her as a casket of jewels. Several of my father's baby teeth, enclosed in a finely crocheted bag, nestled alongside the handkerchiefs in the sideboard drawer, and Tom's first curls had been lovingly pressed between the leaves of the large Family Bible.

The taste of Grandma Leather's delectable lemon cakes is a lasting memory, light as thistledown, tangy with real lemon, they disappeared effortlessly down our throats. Such delicious confections emerged unceasingly from the oven attached to the black cast-iron range along with more robust meals of stew and dumplings, hot-pots and richly-crusted pies. The family were well fed, but only grandma grew fat. Her death, when I was eight years old, came suddenly and unexpectedly. I missed her. But most of all I missed those unforgettable lemon sponge cakes.

Grandpa Leather, as a postman, rose at first light, delivered and collected, and probably sorted, mail all day

25

and retired to bed at dusk. I have no recollection of ever having a conversation with him, but then, he saw more of Gordon than he did of me.

My father, happy to take on board my mother's family, sometimes at the expense of his own, pursued his work and home life, keeping in touch with his parents and brother at decent intervals.

Relatives on my father's side were thin on the ground. Apart from Tom and his wife, Alice, he only managed to rustle up a clutch of cousins in Shropshire — Will, Polly and Marion. One summer in the '30s we visited them and stayed a night. Their cottage, deep in the country-side fulfilled all mother's expectations of what country living should be. She floated in a seventh heaven. There was sunshine, a seat in the shade of a tree and the soft scents and sounds found only in a cottage garden at the height of summer. And then, a smiling Polly, in a pretty print dress, tripping down the garden path with a tray of home-made lemonade and biscuits crusted with icing, provided the crowning touch.

Will spent his working life as a wheelwright and his leisure time as a keen amateur gardener. His cabbages covered the soil like full moons, his leeks grew straight and sturdy as lamp-posts and he sent us staggering home beneath bags of home-grown vegetables, fruit and flowers, the like of which we had never before experienced. Polly kept house for Will. They were a cheerful couple. Marion, too, was a housekeeper, for a pawnbroker in Oldham. When we visited Shrewsbury, Marion arrived soon after us. She had taken her monthly day off to come and make our acquaintance. Temperamentally she was quieter than Will and Polly, timid, fragile and introverted. Over Polly's posh potato pie dinner, Marion disclosed a nugget of information which did not endear her to my mother. Quivering with emotion she revealed that her conscience would not allow her to retire to bed at night until she had spread a meal of cheese and cake crumbs on the kitchen floor for the mice. It probably never occurred to Marion's tender mind that anyone could dislike these small creatures. Unfortunately for her, my mother hated them and Marion's innocent revelation established her as an eccentric in mother's mind. Having made that judgment, it became as irreversible as the law of the Medes and Persians. Though tender-hearted my mother had one or two deep-seated prejudices.

Our short stay with Will and Polly was not repeated. They had an invitation to visit us but failed to take it up. Undismayed my mother said she realised that Will and Polly led such a blissful life in their cottage at Shrewsbury they could not bear to leave it. It seemed a pity. The only relatives my father managed to muster, drifted out of our lives after a single meeting.

Of course, we saw Uncle Tom and Aunty Alice. Though childless, they reared their niece, Hilda, as their own. She was a few years older than me and appeared worldly wise in my eyes. Black-haired, black-eyed, a frail pale girl, Hilda had short-lived surges of energy. Mostly she seemed committed to imparting doom-laden messages, like an undercover agent, in whispered asides, scribbled notes surreptitiously delivered, and a variety of facial contortions suitable to the nature of the news. Placing her hand in front of her mouth, she hissed in my ear one day: "Read this," slipping a folded scrap of paper into my dress pocket. Intrigued, I opened it out and read: 'Your red cheeks and creamy skin mean you are bound to get galloping consumphshun. You will probably die before you're 21.'

I glanced up to see her grinning and grimacing with mock sympathy. Something stirred me to retaliate with:"I don't believe you."

"It's true," she mouthed, morbidly lowering her eyelids. I felt sick.

The conviction that everyone must be aware of an expiry date written all over my face persisted for days. I had nightmares.

"Take no notice of what Hilda says," was my mother's advice, but it did not help. Mother patiently weathered the misery before settling on a practical solution. Early one morning she unfolded the Singer sewing machine and 'ran up' a cotton dress from a generous remnant she discovered in her 'material' drawer. She treadled long and hard. By late evening the last press-stud snapped into place. The bright blue cornflowers printed on a white background were eye catching and pretty. My delight at being allowed to wear the new frock to school next day completely banished Hilda's demoralising prognostications from my mind. I adored my cornflower dress. Life was well worth living after all.

CHAPTER 3

The Corkhills

My mother's sisters, Elizabeth and Ellen, were a constant source of wonderment to me as a child. They possessed an unfailing exuberance for life which added an enduring dimension of pure pleasure to my early years.

Their thoroughbred working-class background guaranteed an abundance of resourcefulness and common sense which swept them along on a full tide of confidence.

Elizabeth Sarah Allinson, generously proportioned with a 42-inch bust and well-rounded hips, had a loud infectious laugh and acute sense of the ridiculous. Her flair for extracting humour out of every situation meant even a calamity could be reduced to manageable proportions. In the most trying circumstances she invariably stayed sanguine. Life was never dull in Aunty Lizzie's company.

There was, however, a price to be paid for this extrovert ebullience. Her mercurial temperament caused her bouts of dyspepsia, heartburn and occasional bilious attacks. Wherever she went her capacious handbag accompanied her, bulging with every conceivable brand of patent medicine and pills for swift relief. The high colour in her cheeks mother described as 'hectic'. Yet her unquenchable zest for life and sharp sense of humour bubbled through all her discomforts and her dark eyes sparkled with fun, most of the time.

Married life, for Aunty Lizzie, began in America. Early in 1912 she sailed across the Atlantic and married Arnold Corkhill in Cincinnati in March of that year. Before going West, Arnold, having served his apprenticeship as a joiner in Bolton, became engaged to Aunty Lizzie. He sent for her to make the journey to Cincinnatti once his fortunes had prospered sufficiently. They had two sons Arnold and Raymond and took out American citizenship.

In 1919, Aunty Lizzie was half-heartedly singing the 'Star Spangled Banner' and wavering about settling permanently in the States. Although her sister Emily and husband, Jack Mumford, had emigrated along with Aunty Lizzie and lived in Chicago, the distance between the two places seemed so immense their meetings could only be infrequent. Aunty Lizzie missed her family in Bolton more and more. Uncle Arnold, aware of her indecision, left the choice entirely in her hands. America or England, he was happy with either.

The dithering continued until a small, but illuminating, incident occurred which settled the issue.

Aunty Lizzie, doing things the American way, stored her flour in a deep bin the size of a barrel. Finding it almost empty one day she decided to clean it out completely. Arnold and Raymond were happily occupied playing horses, the favourite game of the moment, galloping round the house snorting and neighing. By chance they cantered into the kitchen as Aunty Lizzie bent deep into the bin, literally scraping the bottom of the barrel. Only her ample posterior was visible. It proved irresistible to the boys. With hands clasped behind their backs, heads lowered and nostrils flaring they charged and butted her. She overbalanced into the bin. Plastered in flour she emerged with her mind made up. The liberal atmosphere of the New World could only be detrimental to the boys' development and behaviour. Home sweet home in England beckoned.

Their return to Bolton in the 1920s, when the shifting economic fortunes of post-First World War Britain were beginning to be felt, caused them little hardship. The American experience had given them financial stability. Uncle Arnold began his own undertaking business. His almost daily duty was to wait on death and he frequently resembled it. He was exceedingly pale, with a bald head supporting a tonsure of fine dark hair with two broad strands spanning the width of his shiny pate like a bridge joining the twin towers of his ears. Nevertheless, he was compact and trim in build with the neat feet of a dancer, a pastime dear to his heart.

Beneath his remote exterior lay a mordant wit which surfaced now and then. In one of his more expansive moods he told us that at one funeral a mourner arrived so late the service had reached the final hymn, and Uncle Arnold was on the point of entering the church to retrieve the coffin.

"Do you think I dare go in?" she asked him. He looked at her witheringly. "Madam," he replied, "you are not at the Theatre Royal now, and this is not a continuous performance."

Another time my mother was amused and astonished to see a notice in the window of his funeral parlour on St. George's Road. In large black letters it proclaimed to every passer-by:

WHY SUFFER THE ILLS OF THIS WORLD
WHEN YOU CAN BE BURIED IN COMFORT
FOR £12.10s?

There was a toughness about him too. He survived rebellions from his employees, censure from relatives of the deceased and endless battles with grave-diggers. At home though he sat and smoked and regularly read thrillers until the small hours. Often when we were there he would withdraw from the conversation almost as though he were an

31

outsider. Most likely he found it an impossibility to compete with Aunty Lizzie's stream of energetic chatter and chose to let it flow round his shiny white head. Also his habit of chain-smoking gave little opportunity for prolonged speech. His smoker's cough, frequent and intense, gave such offence to the neighbours next door they rushed for their pokers to bang on the fire-back as soon as an attack began. Aunty Lizzie seemed quite happy to let this be the only channel of communication between them and the adjoining houses. Uncle Arnold's smoking habits caused Aunty Lizzie mild concern. Her suspicion that he held a lighted cigarette inside his top hat during funerals, surreptitiously drawing on it as he waited for the service to end, was confirmed when she discovered innumerable small burn marks on the inside crown. She pointed out the dangers. He told her to stop fussing.

The inevitable happened of course. An untimely interruption provided an opportunity for the cigarette to burn a hole in the topper. Aunty Lizzie contenting herself with: "I told you it would happen, Arnold" and simply moulded a piece of Wrigley's chewing gum tidily into the space and smothered it with black boot polish. The top hat attended many more funerals before finding its way into the Hippodrome 'prop' box.

Friday night in the Corkhill household was accounts time. Uncle Arnold sat at the dining room table to 'sweat it out', he said. To alleviate this tiresome task Aunty Lizzie placed a glass of port wine beside him while he concentrated on balancing the books. One evening, preoccupied with his work, he stretched out his hand and drank the contents of the ink bottle by mistake. As soon as he realised what had happened he called Aunty Lizzie in from the kitchen.

"I've drunk the ink instead of the port, Lizzie. What shall I do?"

"Well, Arnold," she said, unmoved, "the best thing you can do now is swallow the blotter." And exploded with laughter.

32

Uncle Arnold moved about silently, coming upon people unawares, as though his constant acquaintance with the dead made him ill at ease with the quick. He disliked having to expend himself unnecessarily, following to the letter one of Aunty Lizzie's adages:

'Never stand when you can sit; never sit when you can lie.'

The only time he broke this rule was on the evenings spent at the Palais-de-Danse, where he and Aunty Lizzie became a happy dancing duo. With crisp footwork, light movement and subtle timing Uncle Arnold never flagged. And if Aunty Lizzie didn't quite equal his virtuosity she made up for it in enthusiasm. Not that she always partnered him. Ever on the watch for a well-turned ankle and neat foot Uncle Arnold chose dancing partners from the shoes up, and never forgot a well-formed foot. The '30s were the peak of the Corkhill's dancing years.

As a special treat one Thursday evening my mother took me to the Palais. The Corkhills were billed to give a display of various dances. We sat on the balcony and I watched entranced as they fox-trotted, quick-stepped and polka-ed round the empty ballroom floor. When it came to the final waltz they danced it with the lightness and delicacy of a swirl of snow, melting to a stop as the final note of music died away.

The next afternoon, Aunty Lizzie told us, one of the mourners at a funeral, not too distraught at her grandmother's passing, congratulated Uncle Arnold on his dazzling display at the Palais. For the one and only time in his undertaking career he broke with precedent and smiled as he drove the hearse to Heaton cemetry.

On her return from the States, Aunty Lizzie unconsciously flaunted her acquired Americanisms.

"Say, Maggie," she said to my mother, "I guess I missed you. And is Nelly just fine?"

Or, "Why that's swell. I gotta say Winifred's real cute."

It amused my mother at first to hear such 'alien' expressions, but within a short time her Lancashire accent re-asserted itself and all was well. Uncle Arnold however, retained some American words in his vocabulary and harboured a special disdain for careless abbreviated speech and long flat vowel sounds. Coming to terms with such phrases as:

'Aw, coom in and 'ave a cup o' tay' or 'Yer mun do summat abeawt it,' was anathema to him.

The Corkhills lived on St. Helen's Road at Four Lane Ends. Their life-style differed from ours. They had money and they owned a shiny black Lanchester. At a time when no more than a couple of dozen cars an hour spluttered and backfired along the peripheral roads of Bolton, the possession of a car indicated the Corkhill's superior social status. They were to be seen driving to the Palais-de-Danse, the cinema or the theatre with unfailing regularity. They were avid cinema and theatre goers. On Saturdays it was first house at the Capitol cinema, second house at the Hippodrome or Grand Theatre. Parking presented no problems, it was door to door and no thought of trouble from vandals. Any hazards came from the speed with which Uncle Arnold rushed Aunty Lizzie to the theatre. One evening, after a busy day of housewifery she eased her tired feet into her carpet slippers as she prepared for her evening out and emerged from the Lanchester outside the cinema to find she was still wearing them. Nevertheless, she sauntered into the stalls with great dignity. Another time, as they took their seats in the Dress Circle of the Grand Theatre she slipped off her fur coat to reveal her all-enveloping flowered pinny. Quickly replacing the fur coat she untied her apron and removed the two garments together.

34

A visit to Aunty Lizzie's was something I appreciated: for one thing the tram, and later the trolley bus terminus was immediately outside their front door. The Corkhill's oak door had a distinctive feature I found appealing, an oval coloured glass panel bearing the words:

A. CORKHILL — FUNERAL DIRECTOR.

Their house also boasted a front garden with a limestone rockery. Another attraction was the comfort of their terraced house which was much more lavishly furnished than our own with deep plush armchairs in the living room, a majestic mahogany grandfather clock in the hall, which solemnly ticked the days away and chimed the hours in a deep resonant tone. The Front Room held a variety of splendid pieces of furniture, never, to my knowledge, used, but unfailingly impressive. It remained, like a room in the British Museum, for purposes of viewing only with exhibits to be admired in hushed tones. Gordon christened it the Funeral Parlour. Silent as the grave, dark as a tomb, cold as a sepulchre. The only good thing about the front room was that on really clear days Winter Hill was visible from the window. Cameos of local life frequently enacted outside the window were observed by Aunty Lizzie. Her accounts of these intriguing dramas were razor sharp in detail and embellishment; these continued, with few character changes, for many years, constituting the soap opera of St. Helen's Road, with most of the dialogue gleaned from the corner shop opposite. We grieved and rejoiced over the pains and pleasures of the Four Lane Ends residents, but where truth ended and fantasy began we never really knew as the storyline expanded quite effortlessly under Aunty Lizzie's imaginative guidance.

Aunty Lizzie's kitchen, avant-garde for those days, contained fitted cupboards with doors on ball bearings which sounded like crunching gravel when they slid back and forth.

At the back of the house a small patch of grass constituted the garden and in the centre stood a standard rose tree, cruelly pruned by Uncle Arnold. Apparently he believed plants had as little feeling as his clients.

My main aversion to visiting Aunty Lizzie's stood at the end of the back garden, the tippler, a black shaft with its eternal rushing water and cavernous drop, quite as terrifying as Grandma Allinson's. Opposite this torture chamber was a garden shed with a tiny side window, used for storing tools. This was another source of fear to me. The shed stimulated Raymond's ghoulish imagination. He conjured up stories of coffins and corpses which scared the life out of me and my Macclesfield cousins Ruth and Nora. He spun a yarn about his father leaving a coffin in the shed. During the night Raymond, wakened by loud moaning, slipped out of the house to investigate. The corpse was sitting up in the coffin, its sightless eyes staring through the shed window. Rich in detail and recounted with convincing solemnity, his tales exerted a hypnotic grip and we found ourselves incapable of dismissing them. The Corkhill's garden shed became a repository of terror.

The first visit I paid, alone, to Aunty Lizzie's was one spring day when I was ten years old. Mother, agitated at the prospect of this solo excursion repeated a caring mother's injunctions — "Don't speak to strange men," "Do hold on to your purse," "Make sure you have a clean hankie" and "Watch where you're going". This final instruction came as a warning to beware of bumping into lamp posts, a regular occurrence which, had my mother stopped to consider, stemmed from her uncanny timing of directing a question at me whenever I was within a foot of a gas lamp. By the time I had answered and turned to move on my head and the lamp were destined to clash with painful and disfiguring results. It also conveyed the hint to avoid gazing into shop windows and consequently losing my way to the right trolley bus.

Mother insisted on walking with me to the tram despite my protests. When one came charging down Tonge Moor Road mother hurriedly pressed an envelope into my hand, "For Aunty Lizzie," she said firmly as the conductor called "Hurry up, luv, we 'aven't got all day." As I nipped aboard, mother called "Don't go upstairs, Edna, it's not safe."

"No mother." "Oh...and Edna," I turned briefly, "keep on the sidesett."

At the next stop I scrambled to the top deck. Nothing could be compared with the thrill of swaying dangerously high above the road and gaining a view of the passing scene from a more exciting vantage point. I also read mother's note to Aunty Lizzie.

'Please see E. leaves your house no later than 3.30. Will meet the tram at Tonge Moor Road post Office about 4 o'clock. Tell her to get off there. She's over-excited about travelling on her own and it makes her careless. Come up Friday, Lizzie, if you can.'

In an uncharacteristic assertion of mutiny and independence I tore it into tiny pieces and when I left the tram dropped them in the USED TICKETS box. Anyway having memorised the message I could deliver it in person.

A wonderful welcome awaited me. Perhaps, Aunty Lizzie said, we should send mother a post card by the lunch-time post to say I had arrived safely. She ferreted through a drawer and found a sepia coloured postcard of Daubhill Station. On second thoughts she then decided the card would arrive at George Barton Street about four o'clock by which time I should be home. This reminded me of my mother's letter and I repeated its contents to Aunty Lizzie. The postcard returned to the glory drawer.

While she made a drink I went to feed the rabbits in their mansion of a hutch made from polished coffin wood. Later we broke the sanctity of the front parlour to view

Aunty Lizzie's latest acquisition, a Limoges vase of which she was extremely proud. I found it quite hideous but felt obliged to say otherwise. The overwhelming smell of camphor mothballs which were stowed away down the sides of the sofa and chairs, and scattered round the edges of the carpet, made me feel faint and sick. Fortunately, Aunty Lizzie had the dinner to cook so we soon retreated to the comfort of the living room.

Dinner, I remember, had to be early that day. Uncle Arnold had a funeral at two o'clock. The boys had gone to the U.C.P. cafe in Deansgate for their dinner and then on to the pictures, so there were just the three of us. By noon the table was laid, vegetables boiled briskly on the electric cooker, and only the sausages waited to be fried. Aunty Lizzie always skinned and floured sausages before cooking. This particular day she determined to try out a practical hint gathered from 'Woman's Weekly': by shaking the sausages in a small bag of flour they would be more evenly coated than rolling them on a floured board.

When blue smoke rose from the heated fat in the frying pan, she reached into her cupboard and took down a small white paper bag. In went the sausages for a quick shake, then plopped into the frying pan. Within seconds they had undergone a remarkable colour change — from floury white to phosphorescent green.

"What the Dickens...?" Aunty Lizzie exclaimed grabbing the offending bag and peering into it as though it were filled with dynamite. She stuck her finger into the flour and licked it. "Good heavens, I am a chump. It's my stomach powder!"

Snatched from the pan, the sizzling green sausages were held under the tap, washed, dried, re-floured and returned to a clean pan. By now they were but a shadow of their former plump selves, so a few rashers of bacon were thrown in to add bulk. Wiping her hands on her apron,

38

Aunty Lizzie said, conspiratorially, "Not a word to Uncle Arnold." She studied the frying sausages reproachfully. Then her sense of the ridiculous surfaced, she started to laugh. We both laughed fit to burst.

At twelve-thirty Uncle Arnold appeared, pale and lugubrious, the inevitable Players cigarette smouldering unnoticed in his mouth until he felt the heat close to his lips, when he removed the stub to light another cigarette from it. He inhaled deeply causing a lengthy fit of coughing, which brought the neighbour's poker into action on their fireback. The newly-lit cigarette was half its size by the time the coughing had subsided. He smiled a welcome to me, congratulated me on my enterprising journey to Four Lane Ends and fell silent.

Aunty Lizzie carried the plates of steaming food to the table. This was the moment of truth but we need not have worried. Uncle Arnold doused tomato ketchup liberally over the sausages and bacon with one hand as he stubbed out his cigarette with the other. His taste buds, atrophied beyond redemption, would not have responded had the food been laced with strychnine. As he sliced into his sausages, Aunty Lizzie raised her eyebrows questioningly.

"All right, Arnold?"

"Mm. Very nice," he said absent-mindedly, pulling out a lump of gristle and placing it tidily on the side of his plate.

Throughout the rest of the meal, Aunty Lizzie sustained a lively monologue on the subject of the boys whose only interest, she complained, was to play gramophone records of Bing Crosby. "All that 'boo-boo-booing' gets on my nerves," she said, mimicking the 'boo boo boo' so accurately it raised a pallid smile from Uncle Arnold. When the grandfather clock struck half past one, Uncle Arnold rose neatly from the armchair and disappeared upstairs coming down minutes later attired in funeral garb, frock coat, shiny top hat, black gloves, smiling mournfully through a haze of cigarette smoke. Aunty Lizzie met him at the bottom of the stairs with a clothes brush and lightly dusted the shoulders of his coat, a useless exercise, with no hair he had no dandruff. Then we escorted him to the front door and he drove away still puffing languidly and wearing an expression of suitable sobriety. The hearse back-fired deafeningly at regular intervals as it progressed down St. Helen's Road. "Enough to resurrect the dead," Aunty Lizzie acidly remarked, giving a boisterous laugh.

"We got away with that one all right." Aunty Lizzie sighed with relief as we went back into the house. "I'll have to lie down for a while. All the excitement over the sausages has given me indigestion."

The thought of Aunty Lizzie resting dismayed me. To delay her I said, "My mother says early to bed, early to rise, makes a man healthy, wealthy and wise."

She nodded thoughtfully. "I don't know about that," she said, remembering no doubt, they never retired before midnight, "but a rest in the day keeps the wrinkles at bay."

"I haven't heard that before."

"You won't have." Aunty Lizzie gave an effervescent chuckle. "I just made it up. And did you know," she added, still laughing at her ingenuity, "that an apple..."

"...a day keeps the doctor away," I interrupted.

"No," she corrected me, "An apple is gold in the morning, silver in the afternoon and lead at night."

"I haven't heard that either." I felt deflated.

"Oh it's a fact, I didn't invent that one. Would you like an apple? Help yourself."

With that she gathered up her feet on to the couch closed her eyes and slept. I read the boys' comics and watched the clock. After half an hour I crept into the kitchen and put the kettle on for a cup of tea. The noise disturbed her. She came into the kitchen smoothing her dress and tucking in vagrant wisps of hair which had escaped her sausage roll style of hairdo. "I feel better for that. The indegestion's gone. I'll brew the tea while you go to the 'doings' — you know." I did know.

40

"I don't want to go," I said decisively.

"Oh but you must," she insisted. "we don't want any wet knickers." She laughed.

"I'll be all right, thank you, Aunty Lizzie."

"Well, if you're sure..."

As the mother of two robust boys, I knew she would never understand my fears of falling down the black hole or facing the spectacle of a corpse grinning at me through the shed window.

She took me across to the trolley bus when it was time for me to leave.

"Come again soon," she called as the bus gave a pneumatic sigh ready for departure. "Next time we'll do something different."

I nodded, feeling somehow disappointed. My initial enthusiasm for the day had evaporated. And all because Aunty Lizzie had slept.

In the 1920s Bolton was known as the Geneva of the North, because of its preponderance of churches and chapels. But the 'opium of the people' as Karl Marx dubbed the influence of religion, gradually faded with the arrival of talking pictures in the '30s. They hypnotised the working people, taking them into a world of fantasy and make believe so far removed from their own and so unattainable that their appeal never faltered. People from all groups and social strata developed an insatiable appetite for the 'Picture Houses' which provided a channel of escapism, previously unknown.

As an inveterate cinema-goer, Aunty Lizzie often went to afternoon shows. Six days a week from one-thirty pm to ten or ten-thirty pm the projectors rolled continuously. For those with sufficient stamina it was

41

possible, for sixpence (2½p), to remain in the cinema from opening to closing time and see the Big Film three or four times.

One autumn day when I was recuperating from some minor illness, Aunty Lizzie arrived and offered to take me to the Capitol for the matinee. "It'll buck her up," she said briskly to mother. Reluctantly, since she disapproved of day-time cinema, mother agreed.

We settled into our sixpenny seats in the middle of a row. Aunty Lizzie heaved a sigh of relief at taking the weight off her feet. Suddenly a man behind us tapped her on the shoulder.

"Take yer 'at off Missus," he hissed, "yor blockin' mi view o't' screen."

Swivelling her head round she gave him a ferocious stare, before slowly removing her felt hat. The performance began. To add to our afternoon's pleasure Aunty Lizzie produced a bag of mis-shapen chocs, cheaper than perfects but equally good. We became engrossed. The chocs rapidly disappeared. The Big Film provided a fantasy so enthralling it was like being shaken awake from a fascinating dream when the man sitting next to Aunty Lizzie jumped up without warning and crashed along the row shouting "Jesus Christ!" He ran, cursing wildly, up the aisle and out of the cinema. Behind us we heard 'shushings' and stage whispers of 'what's up?'

"What is it?" I whispered giving Aunty Lizzie a nudge.

"Just a little excitement," she said. "I'll tell you later."

The man who had demanded the removal of Aunty Lizzie's hat leaned forward menacingly.

"Put a sock in it you blitherin' idiots. Let's have some peace."

Aunty Lizzie looked resolutely ahead. Then the wavering beam of the usherette's torch began its journey from the front row up the aisle to investigate the disturbance. Aunty Lizzie leaned towards me.

"Shall we go?"

Our man behind answered for me.

"Yes. Sling your 'ook and good riddance. We've been saddled with you long enough."

By now the film had lost its appeal and all the chocolates were eaten. We mustered our dignity and belongings and left, to deafening sighs of relief.

Once we reached the comparative peace of the foyer, Aunty Lizzie explained what had happened. Absorbed though she was in the film a sudden movement below her knee distracted her. A hand began making stealthy progress beneath her skirt from calf to knee, then with increasing speed and confidence along her thigh. Some positive action had to be taken. Her hat, balancing on her lap, provided the perfect ammunition for this alarming assault. Calmly removing the four-inch chrome hatpin from its crown, she plunged it deep into the wandering hand, now almost at its journey's end.

"And did it give you heartburn?" I asked wide-eyed and wondering how such a nasty thing could happen at the pictures.

"No," she said with some surprise. "Still now you've mentioned it I'll take a tablet. Stop it before it starts."

Aunty Lizzie accompanied me home. She re-told the afternoon's adventures to my mother's amazement. Although my mother felt such things were not for the ears of a child. Aunty Lizzie nonetheless continued her account with such sparkling humour and vivacity we were all aching with laughter at the end of it.

The next day mother went into town and bought three hatpins from Whitaker's. I watched her fasten them behind the lapels of my coat, blazer and gabardine.

"Be prepared..." she said vaguely.

"For what?" I asked genuinely puzzled.

43

"Well...because...you never know. Think of Aunty Lizzie. Better to be safe than sorry."

I understood, imperfectly.

The story of our afternoon at the pictures recounted by Aunty Lizzie at sundry times tended to expand with graphic embellishments at each telling, one wayward hand became two, her assailant grew in stature from medium height to over six-feet tall; and the hatpin, for those with expansive imaginations like hers, took on the proportions of a dagger.

None of us gave a thought to the fact that a hatpin could be construed as an offensive weapon.

CHAPTER 4

The Johnsons

Strawberry blonde hair singled out Ellen from the rest of the Allinson flock. Her hair was her crowning glory and grey hairs never had the temerity to invade the gold. Every Friday she rinsed her long tresses in vinegar to keep them silky and shining and their colour true. Apart from her hair, Ellen bore the Allinson characteristics of an oval face and brown eyes. Temperamentally she was as spirited and lively as her sisters.

As the youngest member of the family Ellen enjoyed a golden childhood compared with that of her sisters and brothers, being spared the harsher realities of life by doting parents and siblings. Nevertheless she found herself in charge of two looms at the mill before her thirteenth birthday.

Ellen possessed an engaging naivety and candour which endeared her to all the family. Her warm and affectionate nature made her my favourite aunt. I loved Aunty Nellie unreservedly, and I believe the sentiment was mutual. The adults however, noted one outstanding fault, a tendency to pontificate on many matters pertaining to life in general and the subject of health in particular. Assertions on the diagnosis, treatment and prognosis of every ailment fell so forcibly from her lips that contradiction was out of the question. The family, torn between exasperation and resignation when she wore her narrow-eyed look and proceeded to give her considered opinion on the illness under review, ignored the proffered advice, knowing she would eventually wind down. Though acknowledging her pronouncements could be sound, they rarely acted upon them which seemed a shame after all the trouble she took in explaining the necessary steps that ought to be taken in bringing about a full recovery. For good measure, she sometimes threw in a timely aphorism of her own invention, such as, 'A dose in time saves nine', thus neatly wrapping up an unsolicited consultation.

Yet we held her in deep affection. Whenever we landed on her doorstep, either by arrangement or unexpectedly, the genuine delight she expressed at seeing us never wavered.

"Well come on in," she'd say, her voice light with laughter, "I was just thinking about you. I'll make a cup of tea. The kettle's on the boil." And she hastily set about clearing a chair or two so we could sit down. Recognising she had this propensity for untidiness, moved her to apologise effusively for it without making her one whit determined to alter her ways. Piles of ironing — done and waiting to be done, heaps of knitting, bundles of newspapers and mounds of paper flowers covered and spilled over every available flat surface above floor level. When we appeared she cheerfully gathered up the clutter from chairs and tables and transferred them to the already overloaded sideboard. On the occasions she expected us for Sunday tea the living room was miraculously tidy and shipshape. She had managed, somehow, to remove mountains. Exactly where they went we never discovered.

Uncle Samuel Johnson — his parents were devotees of the great doctor — tolerated the turmoil with great good humour. Physically large, fair haired and ruddy faced, his

46

guardsman's bearing created an air of confidence about him which people respected. He held principles of behaviour which he refused to compromise. He always stressed the importance of respect for the dead. In the 1920s and 1930s at 11 am on November 11th all the traffic in town came to a halt, shops stopped serving customers, mill looms remained unattended and school children stood still for two minutes in remembrance of the dead in World War One. The Town Hall clock could be heard striking 11 in every district within four miles of Bolton. Uncle Sam honoured this commitment throughout his life and whenever he saw a funeral passing he stood still and removed his hat in deference to the dead. He maintained it gave comfort to the bereaved.

His duties as an Inspector on Bolton's trams consisted of leaping from one tram to another on various routes, checking passengers' tickets and preventing any attempt at fraudulent conversion of fares in relation to the number of tickets issued. Was the tram running on time? If not, why not? To these responsibilities Uncle Sam added a self-imposed duty, that of inspecting the tram driver. He maintained a driver needed to be physically strong and fearless and unlikely to desert his post in the event of a tram precipitating itself down a broo at breakneck speed and parting company with the tram lines. When we questioned him about this exciting possibility he laughed and said he never stayed on the tram long enough to find out.

The days he plied the Tonge Moor route he alighted at the Starkie Arms and visited us. He carried messages between Aunty Nellie and my mother. As an intermediary in communications, Uncle Sam showed the patience of Job. Theirs was an immortal language he painstakingly learnt to decipher over the years. He repeated the essence of Aunty Nellie's instructions correctly and cryptically, having evolved his own verbal shorthand. Thus her long-winded arrangement for an afternoon meeting with my mother emerged from Uncle Sam as *"Tognarelli's at 2. Bring E., blue brooch, No. 10 needles, Florrie's Scripture Cake recipe, Arthur's sock."*

In his navy blue inspector's uniform he resembled a jovial John Bull. He worked early, day and evening shifts. This discouraged Aunty Nellie from cultivating a regular routine and often she became so engrossed in her knitting or creating paper flowers that Uncle Sam's arrival, though anticipated, threw her into a flurry of activity which eventually concluded with an appetising meal.

"Your tea won't be many minutes, Sam," she'd say with a lively confidence while her mind raced through the contents of the meatsafe hoping to alight on a tasty morsel she could rustle up into a satisfying meal for a well-built man of healthy appetite. The delightful, unique shambles of her kitchen was far removed from the well-ordered, cupboarded kitchen of Aunty Lizzie and ingredients had to be hunted down with all the ingenuity of a sleuth searching for vital clues.

Uncle Sam never complained. After clearing a pile of paraphenalia from a chair he would sit down, smoke a cigarette or two and wait patiently until the food appeared. Mostly he ate alone, Aunty Nellie and Winifred taking their meals at regular times, but it savoured of a social occasion through the channel of conversation. Theirs was a communicative household. Over a mug of steaming tea Aunty Nellie discussed the day's events, asked advice on any problems and together they resolved them during Uncle Sam's evening meal. His digestion was of the best. Even when the legs at his end of the table sank unexpectedly through the floor one day, he showed no alarm but captured his sliding plate and pot of tea and calmly finished the remains of his meal, before investigating the extent of the wet rot in the floorboards. His calmness balanced Aunty Nellie's nervous apprehension.

My cousin, Winifred, fashioned from the neatest mould, possessed all the attractive physical attributes I lacked. Rich brown curls, a skin that turned honey gold in the sun and a small mouth that constantly curled upwards in smiles. We became constant companions during our childhood years. She was two years my junior and an only child. This made Aunty Nellie over-protective at times.

Winifred attended Devonshire Road school and her mother accompanied her there and back for so many years it became embarrassing. Then at eight-years old, Winifred with that infant determination which mothers ignore at their peril, put her sturdy little foot down and announced, 'I am going to school and coming home by myself. Everyone else does.'

Her mother, recognising a familial stubbornness, capitulated, with great reluctance. For many months after this she stationed herself at the front gate when Winifred left for the 250 yards journey to school. As lunch time approached she re-positioned herself at a suitable vantage point greeting Winifred as though she was returning from a long and hazardous safari. The schedule was repeated in the afternoon. In between times, Aunty Nellie fraught with anxiety indulged the Allinson habit of worrying. My aunts and mother were born worriers. Their capacity for worrying caused them much concern. Their lives were spent in fear and trepidation that disasters might happen. They never did. On the rare occasions when they acknowledged life was not presenting any problems they became distressed about the absence of something to worry about. So then they worried about each other. Positive thinking, even if it had been invented then, would not have dented their armour of worry. Mother once said to Aunty Nellie, 'You know Nellie, I'm worried about how much I worry.' To which Aunty Nellie gave the classic reply. 'Yes, it bothers me, Maggie, how much you worry. In fact, it more than bothers me, it worries me.' Between them my aunts and my mother elevated their perpetual state of worry to an art form in itself.

The Johnson home in Lonsdale Road, a cottage terrace house much lighter than most, had a deep vestibule which served both as a barrier between them and unwanted callers and a draught excluder. At the front was a small neat garden. Directly opposite the house stood St. Margaret's Church where they attended Matins regularly. With all of ten yards to walk to the church gate, they invariably arrived as the opening hymn ended.

Inside number 35, the front room smelled richly of Mansion polish and the linen in the sideboard drawers held the tangy fragrance of White Windsor soap. But above all, I associate Aunty Nellie and number 35 Lonsdale Road with the distinctive smell of Pears Soap which she used throughout her lifetime.

However, my mother regarded Aunty Nellie's haphazard routine as a fruitless toil when, she believed, with a modicum of organisation, her days could have been more productive. The trouble was, my mother always harboured a sense of protective responsibility towards her youngest sister which inclined her to interference.

It is true Aunty Nellie diversified the tasks of the day to such an extent she created more jobs than she could adequately cope with. She did a little of everything somewhat on the principle of looking after the pennies and allowing the pounds to look after themselves. Before clearing the breakfast dishes ten rows of knitting had to be completed. Then the dilemma arose whether to 'wash up, do a bit of baking, washing, cleaning or shopping' as she put it. Decisions were adjourned indefinitely so that the remnants of half-finished chores piled up relentlessly and grew into a glorious muddle. In between times she sat down with a cup of tea.

There are only two occasions I recall clearly when my mother felt at her wits' end through what she believed was Aunty Nellie's, and her own, lack of structured action in one case and lack of foresight on Aunty Nellie's part in the other.

The first concerned a holiday. Winifred had been ill with scarlet fever. The doctor recommended convalescence. The arrangements were that Aunty Nellie and Winifred should stay with us for one week then go to Bispham for a few days.

Uncle Sam, as an honoured employee of Bolton Transport Department delegated one of their drivers to take Aunty Nellie and Winifred in a car to Bispham. The car duly arrived on the Saturday morning, a 1928 Ford. Our house had been chaotic during the packing. It was early May: 'cast not a clout till May is out' Aunty Nellie repeated at regular intervals, so woollies were thrown in along with cotton dresses and Winifred's rubber wading shoes. Finally their suitcases were shut and deposited by the front door. Their macs were flung over them. Mother, noticing unsightly bulges, investigated. The pockets were stuffed with long knitted scarves.

As a sisterly gesture, mother had prepared food sufficient to last until their return home. Among the goodies in the deep oval basket were tins of salmon and fruit, biscuits and fruit cake. A roasted leg of lamb, packed separately, lay beside the basket.

The cases were stowed in the car boot and fond farewells ensued. Mr. Kendal helped Winifred into the back of the car before sliding into the driving seat. Aunty Nellie carrying the basket and carrier bag of lamb, ran round to the other rear door and climbed in beside Winifred. The engine started, cut out, fired and backfired before moving off still making a noise like rapid gunfire. Pale faces appeared at the windows. The cherries on Aunty Nellie's hat trembled with the vibration. One gloved hand waved regally.

"Have a good time", we shouted cheerily. They could not hear above the noise of the engine, but kept on waving until they disappeared from view.

Next morning a postcard from Bispham dropped on our doormat. Unlike Aunty Nellie's usual ramblings the message was succinct:

'Leg of lamb missing. Left on running board. Must have fallen off. Please forward if found. N. & W.'

Mother turned white. The loss seemed unbelievable. Her silence spoke volumes.

The second incident happened one sunny Spring day. At the height of the drama, mother and I were swaying into Bolton on the tram. Our destination happened to be Aunty Nellie's. My desire to show off my chicken-pox scars had prompted the spur of the moment decision. We arrived in time to marvel at the miracle of Aunty Nellie's deliverance.

A splodge of bird-lime on the outside of the front bedroom window instigated the afternoon's events. The bird-lime offended Aunty Nellie's sense of hygiene and cleanliness. It would be but the work of a moment to raise the lower sash window, hoist herself onto the ledge outside, manoeuvre the window into position and remove the deposit with the 'chammy' leather. So the afternoon's drama began. First she lifted the window sufficiently to allow her to lean out and scan the street for signs of life. Nothing moved in the warm afternoon sun. The window, pushed up to its full extent, allowed plenty of space for her to climb out and seat herself firmly on the ledge. Her legs dangled inside the bedroom. The leather lay damply beside her. She tugged at the window but it refused to budge. Placing both hands under it she gave a gentle shake. Then more vigorously. Without warning the sash cord snapped. Down crashed the window trapping both hands between it and her legs. She felt faint. Desperately she called for help to the silent street. Nothing and no-one stirred; not even the Holden's cat was abroad. Time passed and the sun shone hotly. Aunty Nellie prayed for a merciful release. Eventually it came in the form of Mr. Milner from next door, but one.

She heard him open his front door and gazed down dizzily. Absorbed in stabbing his tobacco into the bowl of his

52

pipe he failed to notice her. After three feeble attempts to attract his attention, Mr. Milner at last looked up. He was a benign man but not noted for speed and agility.

"Good laws, Mrs. Johnson," he exclaimed in surprise, "what are thi doin' up there?"

"The sash window's fallen on my hands. I can't move. Get me out."

Mr. Milner drew deeply on his pipe while he contemplated how best such a hefty operation might be undertaken. As a retired joiner he was well acquainted with the vagaries of sash windows. However, his strength was on the wane.

"Hang on," he said unnecessarily, "I'll fetch someone to help me."

"Then look sharp about it," Aunty Nellie said tartly, though with the advent of a saviour, even if it was only in the short form of Mr. Milner, her spirits revived. Finding a young, strong assistant took Mr. Milner some time. He finally located a handsome curly-haired plumber working at number 19. They stood in Aunty Nellie's garden debating tactical manoeuvres with infuriating patience.

Aunty Nellie growing desperate called, "Hurry up, Mr. Milner. HURRY UP." Mr. Milner recommended restraint.

"Don't fret yourself, Mrs. Johnson," he said soothingly, "we're on our way." His pipe went out. He banged out the ash and prepared for a refill. Aunty Nellie swayed with faintness. Her mouth became bone dry. She felt like throwing a fit of hysterics. Instead she pleaded with him to desist.

"Patience, Mrs. Johnson," Mr. Milner remonstrated, though he did put the unfilled pipe in his pocket. "Keep your pecker up. We're coming."

"Well, get a move on. I've had enough. The back door's unlocked."

She felt rivulets of perspiration trickling down her face and neck. Her hair plastered itself to her head. Mr. Milner and the plumber disappeared.

By now, a knot of curious neighbours had gathered on the pavement, craning their necks and dispensing pointless advice and encouragement.

"Keep your head, Mrs. Johnson, and you'll land on your feet."

"To say you've been there so long, Mrs. Johnson, you're not doing so badly."

"Don't let it upset you, Nellie." This from her next door neighbour, Mrs. Singleton. "Shall we come up?" Aunty Nellie's reply was terse. "No thank you."

"Feather brained interferers," she said later. "I didn't want them nosey parkering round my upstairs." All her concentration centred on the bedroom door, waiting for the appearance of her rescuers. The sound of heavy footsteps laboriously scaling the stairs was sweet music to her. But she could hardly believe her ears when they tapped politely on the door, before creeping in like a couple of intruders rather than heroes of the hour. If the situation had not been so desperate she told us she would have asked them to take off their boots. They trod delicately across the bedroom and eyed her through the window.

"This is Joe," Mr. Milner said, jerking his head at his smiling companion, "he's doin' a plumbin' job lower down the street." He was making a brave attempt to take Aunty Nellie's mind off her miserable situation. "He favours J. R. Smith, don't you think?" She looked blank. "You know, Mrs. Johnson, the great Bolton Wanderers' player."

Aunty Nellie, past thinking and beyond words, groaned. Her feelings towards Mr. Milner grew less benevolent by the minute. His hand wandered to his jacket pocket for his pipe but catching Aunty Nellie's look of anguish thought better of it. "We'll have you inside in a jiffy." He glanced down at her dangling feet. "Keep your trotters movin' Mrs. Johnson, it'll help your circulation." He turned to Joe. "We'll just do a bit of cogitatin'". The prospect of swift rescue remained tantalisingly out of reach.

From the depths of his plumber's overalls, Joe suggested jacking up the window, not too suddenly though in case Mrs. Johnson fell backwards and flattened her patch of pansies.

Aunty Nellie weak with pain and heat observed their deliberations in an agony of suspense. Their puzzled looks gave her cold comfort.

Mr. Milner thought perhaps the Fire Brigade should be called. The effect on Aunty Nellie was as sensational as forked lightning. "Are you mad, Mr. Milner...or am I?"

At this point we appeared at the bedroom door. The dispiriting sight of Aunty Nellie framed in the window, produced an anguished "Well, what's to do?" from my mother and a rush of tears from Aunty Nellie. Mother, too, would have succumbed to weeping had she not felt impelled to swift action. She had the men organised in moments.

"Bring the clothes prop from the backyard," she ordered Joe. While he crashed downstairs to get it, Mr. Milner and mother slid an arm either side of Aunty Nellie and linked hands behind her back. Gingerly I held her ankles which had swollen alarmingly. Mr. Milner, a past master of unnecessary remarks said, "Ready when you are, Mrs. Johnson." Joe jacked up the window with the prop, held it fast and, slowly and painfully Aunty Nellie was eased into the bedroom.

Outside, a faint cheer rose from the onlookers that put paid to Aunty Nellie's tears. "Shiftless lot," she said, with a return to her usual robustness, "nothing better to do."

"There's one thing," Mr. Milner remarked tactlessly as Aunty Nellie finally touched down on the bedroom floor. "You're very well upholstered, Mrs. Johnson, otherwise it could have been a good deal worse." And Joe, anxious to add his own contribution to the success of the operation added, "Well, you couldn't have had a finer day for it."

Aunty Nellie managed a feeble laugh of relief and attempted to stand. Her legs buckled. Mr. Milner and Joe supported her to the bed. Her hands had doubled their bulk like well-risen dough.

Mother took charge. Joe, half-a-crown better off, and now surplus to requirements returned to unblock U-bends and waste pipes at number 19. Mr. Milner relaxed, re-loaded his pipe, lit it, and puffing contentedly pottered off to buy a new sash cord. He repaired the window free of charge.

After a shot of brandy, the infallible antidote for shock, Aunty Nellie bumped downstairs on her backside holding her hands out like a sleepwalker. Mother applied bi-carbonate of soda paste to both hands after bathing them in hot and cold water. She wondered if any bones were broken and hinted that a visit to Bolton Royal casualty department might be advisable. The heroic survivor would not entertain the idea. Perhaps call the doctor then? An emphatic "No" silenced us all. "I'll be as right as rain in the morning."

Mrs. Singleton was despatched to collect Winifred from school and break the news of her mother's accident.

Laughter began to surge back into the conversation as Aunty Nellie told us what had happened. Then the vicar called having bumped into Mrs. Singleton up the road. With careless indifference he dropped his panama hat on a heap of Aunty Nellie's painstakingly sculpted paper carnations. She winced as her creations disappeared beneath a hat which had so recently housed the Rev. Gibson's bald head. Interpreting this as a sign of acute pain he fell to his knees and offered a prayer pleading a speedy recovery and adding a codicil of thanks for safe deliverance. He left cherishing the hope Aunty Nellie might soon find the strength to cross the road to St. Margaret's and attend Sunday morning service.

Winifred flew in the back door, burst into tears on seeing her mother incapacitated and remained inconsolable, until her mother and mine assured her that death was not imminent.

Comfrey root, applied liberally inside and out worked wonders. My mother cooked Uncle Sam's tea. He happened to be on day shift and arrived home soon after. He commiserated. We left as the twice-told tale unfolded with intricate exaggeration. A post card informed Aunty Lizzie of the situation. We dropped it in the post-box on our way home.

My mother attempted, through gentle persuasion, to extract assurances from her sister that she would confine her window cleaning to inside the house in future. But it failed. If Aunty Nellie experienced small stabs of guilt about the episode she never admitted to them and promptly changed the subject.

Within a week she was spotted sitting on the window ledge scraping off the bird-lime, now securely stuck to the pane. Mother remonstrated but her words fell on deaf ears.

"I'll never fathom Nellie," she said resignedly.

CHAPTER 5

An ill wind

For several days Gordon had been off colour. Any interruptions in the rhythm of our days came mainly from illness. Our health was mother's principal consideration. Contemplating the incalculable number of diseases our flesh was heir to set her leafing through her books of herbal remedies and concocting a few of her own. Yet we succumbed, despite her perpetual vigilance, to all the infectious diseases plus other unspecified ailments such as 'growing pains', inexplicable lassitude, headaches and 'funny turns'.

Smitten with mumps, our necks and jaws firmly bound with flannel made drinking through a straw hazardous, and choking a distinct possibility. When we went down with measles the house curtains stayed tightly closed for a week as a precaution against blindness. The summer we caught chicken-pox we looked for all the world like a couple of clowns with faces plastered in bi-carbonate of soda paste to prevent scratching of spots which might leave scars. And when we developed whooping cough we all but died.

Fortunately our parents kept fit. As far as I recall my mother never suffered from any illness which required her to stay in bed and my father developed a chesty cold and cough only about once a year. At the first hint of this annual event he took to his bed for a couple of days, savouring the care and attention which put him back on his feet ready for work on the third day.

During the 1920s and 1930s the scourge of T.B. was truly a force to be reckoned with. 'Drink plenty of milk' became the general advice of the health experts in an effort to build up our bodies' resistance to this frequently fatal disease. Our milkman, Mr. Lowe made a twice daily round with his horse-drawn float listing to starboard with milk-filled galvanised metal churns, their lids tipped to an angle by the dangling ladles. On cold mornings his horse, anxious to be on the move, snorted, blowing steamy clouds of warm breath from its nostrils as Mr.Lowe ladled streams of creamy liquid into our jugs where it frothed and bubbled as though it were the elixir of life. In fact it probably seethed with germs. In summer the milk went off within a couple of days or settled on top of one's tea in small white flecks. This, Aunty Nellie declared, was often a sign of thunder in the air.'

Pneumonia also took its toll. With no antibiotics, the treatment at home relied on bread poultices, antiphlogistine and unremitting nursing care. The 'crisis', reached after three days was the crucial turning point and when successfully overcome, recovery was assured. But all too often the patient yielded to the crisis with fatal results. The dread of these afflictions kept my mother in a constant state of watchfulness not to mention worry on our behalf.

'HOME MADE MEALS' could well have replaced 'BLESS THIS HOUSE' as the embroidered text hanging on the wall beside the fireplace. My mother had a deep suspicion of bought food and hardly had a good word for the fish and chip shop or meat pies from any shop. "They're bad for you. Very indigestible," she argued when we pleaded. So of course, we loved them all the more. When, on rare occasions, inventiveness deserted her she would light the oven, put the kettle on, throw the cloth over the kitchen table and sit down to ponder. We waited with mounting excitement. If inspiration continued to elude her, she stood up, straightened her apron and said in tones of martyrdom, "What is it to be, fish and chips or meat pies?" This admission of defeat sent us speeding to the chip shop. However, mother's aversion to fish and chips stopped short at the newspaper in which they were wrapped. If it happened to be the *News of the World* she would smooth it out and put it aside until she had eaten her fish. Then she would read the fascinating snippets of society scandal, and run her eye over mysterious adverts for double trusses, colonic lavage and surgical corsets. "While my chips cool," was her excuse. We devoured our portions and most of her chips too as she became engrossed in her reading. She feigned surprise at seeing her empty plate and, screwing up the newspaper to throw on the fire said with cheery predictability, "Well, I didn't enjoy that meal one bit." Our hearts sank. It would be many a long day before fish and chips came on the menu again.

There were seasonal supplements for our health. In winter Malt Extract or Scott's Emulsion fortified us every day and Fenning's Fever Cure at the first sneeze. Brimstone and treacle purified the blood, and replaced the winter medicines at the first hint that spring was in the air and, in summer, the real treat, fresh orange juice, hand-squeezed each morning. My mother believed implicitly in 'working' medicine in the form of Syrup of Figs, the complete panacea for stubborn or sluggish bowels. Two teaspoonsful were administered every Friday night without fail throughout the year. Swallowing this obnoxious black liquid became a trial of strength for me. With difficulty I managed the first teaspoonful but retched at the second. Gordon swallowing his dose uncomplainingly, gloated accordingly. "You're weak," he said patronisingly and I, wallowing in misery, did not deny it.

Yet despite mother's diligent care the dreaded scourge did not pass us by entirely. Those few days Gordon was off colour he remained unresponsive to every remedy in

my mother's book. Even Fenning's Fever Cure and Little
Lung Healers failed to make any improvement. He suddenly
became feverish and complained of earache. Discovering
several swollen glands in his neck, further self-help seemed
pointless. The doctor was called in.

So when I came home from school one dinner-time I
saw Dr. Douglas stooping over Gordon lying languidly on
the couch. His presence filled the living room. Dr. Douglas,
naturally taciturn and serious, looked grave. He was a tall,
ascetic Scot with a long pale face and searching grey eyes. He
always entered the house unhurriedly, carrying his
stethoscope like a riding whip. Though his manner bordered
on the brusque he excelled as a diagnostician. Gordon and I
trembled at the sight of him. He might have been a vet
examining animals for all the response he elicited from us.
We left the talking to mother, merely nodding or shaking our
heads mutely in response to his rapid questions.

The morning Dr. Douglas visited Gordon was
memorable for the one word I heard him utter — T.B. As he
spelled out the treatment he tapped his stethoscope on the
table. A note was written to be handed in at the Infirmary
Out-Patients' Department. When at last Dr. Douglas
departed my mother said, "I feel as though I've been through
the mangle." She spoke for the three of us.

I was despatched to Mrs. Hamer's at number 29 with
an urgent message to come as soon as possible. Our very
present help in time of trouble was busy making an apple pie
when I arrived but she dropped her rolling pin and hurried
back with me to see what she could do. Mrs. Hamer had
been a nurse when young; now a widow of many years she
spent her time helping the young wives in the Triangle.
Though childless herself, she showed endless patience with
Gordon and me. Calm, practical and utterly reliable her
experience of life smoothed my mother's path on countless
occasions. She was able to reassure my mother that her fears
of dramatic decline and possible death were groundless.
Dr. Douglas's diagnosis of T.B. glands of the neck was

treatable, but it would take time, Mrs. Hamer said with authority. In fact, eighteen months passed before Gordon was discharged by the hospital.

Aunty Nellie was sent for. As the diagnosis, treatment and prognosis had already been determined by the doctor and Mrs. Hamer, she refrained from adding her own thoughts on the future outlook. She whisked me off to Lonsdale Road and I stayed for three weeks, with frequent visits home, until my mother had established a routine of visiting the Infirmary with Gordon daily.

Aunty Nellie's conscientiously created confusion, so unlike our daily round at home appealed to me. No two days were alike and that added spice to life at number 35. The School Board granted a special dispensation for me to attend school during my stay, which caused tears before breakfast from Winifred. She still had five months to her fifth birthday and school was an unattainable goal for her. There were also tears before bedtime. As a concession to my seven years Aunty Nellie allowed me to stay up for half an hour after Winifred went to bed. However, as she spent the 30 minutes at the top of the stairs chanting: "When is Edna coming up?" the pleasure of the extra half hour dwindled rapidly and I took to going to bed at the same time as Winifred.

During my stay in Lonsdale Road Aunty Nellie indulged my every whim with characteristic generosity. She bought me *Chick's Own, Film Fun* and a sherbet, forbidden by my mother, all in one week. I made a rather reluctant return home.

When Aunty Lizzie heard the news she arrived with a basket full of food, cleaned the house from top to bottom, took home the washing and made twice weekly visits until she was convinced my mother could cope. Uncle John bounced in bearing gifts from Aunty Agnes, and Aunty Alice appeared on the doorstep one day with Hilda clutching her hand, looking pale and frightened at the report of 'consumshon' in the family. Aunty Alice took on the

63

responsibility of shopping, though my father said she made heavy weather of buying four flour cakes and half a pound of smoked bacon.

Our safe comfortable world had turned upside down with the onset of Gordon's illness but everyone rallied round and kept the home fires burning. Dr. Douglas appeared at intervals and pronounced himself well pleased with Gordon's progress and towards the end of the hospital treatment he suggested to mother that, whenever possible, she should take Gordon to the country. The windy heights of Belmont or Turton where the air was clear and fresh offered one option. But mother hesitated. It might be beneficial, on the other hand... a sudden chill and the spectre of pneumonia loomed large. Plenty of fresh air and exercise were necessary, she admitted, nevertheless the bleakness of the moors made her shudder as much for her own health as Gordon's.

My father came up with the answer. Through a chance remark to a fellow member of the Royal Order of Foresters, the only association my father ever joined, we heard of the Phillips family at Horwich, where they farmed.

Stoneycroft Farm brought a new and exciting dimension to our lives. Mr. and Mrs. Phillips expressed their willingness to have us at any time. Mother took up the offer and so began a long and happy friendship with a family whose way of life differed from ours in almost every respect.

Years later when I read D. H. Lawrence's 'Sons and Lovers' his description of Mrs. Morel's and Paul's first visit to Willey Farm echoed my memory of our initial excursion to meet the Phillip's family. Mother chose a fine day. When we left the tram at Doffcocker the walk to Stoneycroft Farm seemed like a journey into another world. The path meandered through a copse of richly-leaved trees; a magical place, cool and green in the midst of sun-warmed fields. Then on past two reservoirs leading eventually to a narrow stone-strewn lane up to the farm.

On this July day we came upon Stoneycroft Farm unexpectedly, tucked away in a hollow below the road.

64

Upper windows, thrown wide open, were at eye level and from one of the rooms came the busy whirr of a sewing machine. Dogs barked startling us and two border collies appeared at the corner of the barn. We hesitated. Suddenly a girl's voice, sharp and distinct called from somewhere unseen, "Quiet, Floss. Lie down Laddie," silencing the dogs immediately. We moved across the yard. Unfortunately animals were not a feature of our upbringing, making us apprehensive of them. The Phillips soon changed that.

A pungent scent of roses climbing round the wooden lattice porch drifted towards us. They tumbled in pink profusion round the door and over the walls. Then we spied the doves. Pure white fan-tailed birds coo-ing throatily on the dovecote beyond the farmhouse. At our approach they flew into the air, feathers gleaming in the sunlight, and settled on the barn roof. There they continued to chunter broodingly. No sooty specks marked their purity, or that of the washing which was strung across from barn to house. The sight of such dazzling cleanliness brought a sigh of envy from my mother.

The door stood open. Mrs. Phillips materialised in a flowered pinafore over a short-sleeved dress, plump and pink and smiling. Her hands and forearms, round and strong from years of heaving milk churns and handling children and animals gave an impression of capability and dependability, the archetypal farmer's wife. Behind her, eyeing us with curiosity stood one of her daughters. She looked about 12. "This is Joyce," Mrs. Phillips said by way of introduction. Joyce grinned. The blue eyes behind the owl-like spectacles appeared friendly. We smiled at each other but said nothing. Mrs. Phillips came to the rescue. "Would you like to go up to the hayfield with Joyce and...? She stopped, noticing our town clothes. "Will they be all right?" she asked dubiously, turning to my mother. "They'll probably come back covered in dust and hay."

"Oh, it doesn't matter," mother said airily, "I'll know how to dress them for the country next time," taking it for granted we should be coming again.

Joyce ran ahead of us up the stony lane to a meadow where haymaking was in full swing. Gordon and I hung about the gate watching the men at work while Joyce skipped over to her father. Hardly pausing in his pitching of hay on to the cart, he nevertheless managed to send a friendly acknowledgement of our presence — a short dab at his flat cap with the fork handle, and beckoned us over. Between the cart shafts stood a shire horse, champing resignedly, awaiting the signal to move. "This is Dolly," Joyce said giving the huge neck a fond slap. We tried to absorb the scene, the tractor in the next field spluttered and looped round the field leaving swathes of grass, the haymakers gathering it into heaps while others tossed the gathered mounds on to the cart and the whole operation proceeded with smooth rhythmical movements. This pastoral scene had a settled tranquility about it all as though it encapsulated the whole world and outside of it nothing really existed.

Joyce broke the spell. "You can rake some hay if you like." We did like. Mr. Phillips smiled encouragingly; a short craggy man, brown as a nut, he moved easily with the rhythm of his work. It was as though many seasons had moulded his body to the contours of the countryside.

On top of the haycart his sons, Jack and Harry, stacked the tossed hay. Gordon and I watched spellbound.

While the weather held, every able-bodied soul who offered help was taken on. Joyce told us they would work from dawn to dusk to assist the gathering in of hay from several fields around. We added our feeble efforts striving to work as fast as the others. We sweated and panted, gathered and tossed, loving every heated minute and oblivious to the fact that on the whole we impeded progress rather than reinforced it.

"Want to come up?" Harry shouted. I hung back. The hay looked as high as a mountain. Before I could make up my mind Jack jumped down lifted me in his arms and tossed me like a bale of hay up to Harry. Landing with a soft bounce on the growing stack I found to my surprise that Gordon was already sitting beside me having been given a leg-up by Jack. Now we could help stack the hay. Once the cart carried its full load Harry announced I should have to return to the ground. I wanted to protest but Harry only laughed and dropped me carefully into Jack's waiting arms. Seconds later Gordon launched himself from the top of the cart plummeting with a thud on the stubbly earth. Although he landed on his feet the impact caused his legs to give beneath him and his knees took the brunt of the fall. Cut, bleeding and winded he stood up and said defiantly, "Nothing to it. I could do it again." But Joyce saved him the embarrassment of a repeat performance by dragging a huge wicker hamper full of food and drink, from beneath the hedge. The haymakers downed tools and took a break.

Joyce raced us back to the farm. The dogs barked a welcome, hearing us in the lane and at the farmhouse door stood Rose, her sewing machine abandoned as she joined us for tea. She was grown-up and earned her living from dressmaking. Judging by her clean-cut, well-dressed appearance and fine white hands, Rose spent little time about the farmyard. Her tasks were mainly indoors and concerned with domestic duties. She was tall and slender with a wide smile. Examining the torn hem of my dress with an expert eye she said, "I'll mend that for you after tea."

Tea was a lavish affair. A true farmhouse spread. Good manners forsook me. "I want a piece of fruit cake," I burst out, leaning over the table prepared to help myself. Horrified, my mother caught my hand in mid-stretch. "Just a moment my girl. I want, never gets."

I sighed. "Please may I.....?"

"And thank you," my mother prompted.

"And thank you." Manners seemed such a waste of good eating time. Mrs. Phillips laughed and handed me the two-tier cakestand with its chrome handle stuck through the middle. I chose a generous slice. "Leave room for scones and strawberry jam," she urged, "I'm sure you can manage that."

"Yes." Speaking with my mouth full I choked on a crumb, and splutterings of cake flew out of my mouth.

"Don't speak with your mouth full," mother chipped in pursing her lips with annoyance and, to re-inforce the advice, slapped me on the back with such force more cake crumbs spattered on the tablecloth.

Mrs. Phillips, already spreading jam on buttered scones, turned the attention away from me. "You should be glad her appetite's so good, and Gordon's too." They gazed on him with pleasure as he quietly waded through sandwiches and drop scones leaving me to enjoy every last crumb of cake.

Joyce, whose spectacles continually slipped down her nose giving her a clownish appearance, jumped up from the table as soon as tea ended. "D'ye want to come to the top field and bring the cows down for milking?" Gordon, excited at the prospect, did not need a second bidding. Handing him a stick and calling to the dogs Joyce led the way. I stayed behind to have my dress repaired.

Rose's sewing room held all the paraphernalia of a professional dressmaker — two sewing machines, two tailor's dummies, endless tins of needles and pins, tape measures, French chalk and, best of all, a rich variety of materials. As she stitched my frock I let scraps of silk and satin slip through my fingers. Removing half a dozen pins from between her lips Rose said, "You can keep anything you find on the floor." A swatch of ivory satin caught my eye. I rubbed its shiny smoothness against my cheek. Rose laughed, "Do you like it? It's a piece of material from my wedding dress. You could make a dress for your doll, perhaps."

I collected as much material, lace and ribbon as I could hold. Rose stuffed them in a bag, delighted to see a reasonably tidy floor. My booty would go into the ragbag at home. Rummaging through the ragbag was a favourite pastime on wet days. All its contents were known to my mother who had a memory of every oddment of material it held. Economy inhibited her from throwing anything away and the leftovers from dresses and shirts and blouses she had made went into the ragbag, 'just in case' they might come in useful sometime.

My mother could not resist asking Rose if she felt it unwise to make her own wedding dress. Superstition decreed that to do so was unlucky. Rose shrugged that aside. "I'm making the bridesmaids' dresses too. I can't afford to believe such tales." Mother did not pursue it, she just knew she would not have dreamt of making her own wedding dress and tempt ill-luck anymore than she would put a pair of new shoes on the table for the same superstitious reason.

The wedding, Rose informed us, would be at the end of September after harvest. My mother made a note of it.

Gordon and Joyce had not yet returned with the cows. I hung out of the sewing room window surveying the lane. The late afternoon sun poured over the farmyard and the fields beyond. The doves hovered about the dovecote and the scent of climbing roses drifted up. This was a moment to cherish. It held for a brief instant. Then the whirr of the sewing machine started up behind me. And below, a door opened. Mrs. Phillips emerged carrying a bucket, scattering corn from it among the hens pecking busily around the barn door. She glanced up and smiled. Life was work even in this idyllic setting, and the Phillips' family perpetuated their life with a sense of vocation as strong as the timelessness of the land.

"I've got some eggs and jam for you," Mrs. Phillips called. Rose helped me into my dress and I ran downstairs. Mrs. Phillips stood with my mother in the stone-floored dairy room. A cool place with marble shelves and whitewashed walls. Home-cured hams hung from the ceiling, trays of eggs stretched in massed ranks along the lower shelves, kegs of butter, pans of milk covered with muslin and cheeses filled one side of the room and, on the top shelves, jams and chutneys gave way to bottled fruit. There seemed no end to this garnered harvest. The other face of the dairy scene went unremarked, the fly-papers suspended from the ceiling, black with bluebottles and flies; and the honey jars set as traps to let in the wasps where they drowned in sweetness. The cowpats and horse droppings in the farmyard festered with flies,too, I noticed.

A noise like the sound of discordant trombones heralded the cows' arrival. Joyce manoeuvred them into the shippon as Gordon wielded his stick like a baton trying his best to look professional.

The day had been unforgettable. With our haul of produce we set off home happy to know we could return to this haven of rural peace any time. Exhibiting my unfortunate habit of casual carelessness I realised, when we were about 100 yards down the lane, that my bag of materials had been left behind.

"Your head will never save your legs," my mother remonstrated."Run back. Gordon and I will wait here."

"Can't Gordon go?" I sounded petulant and spoilt.

"No. You can." Mother and Gordon sank onto comfortable flat stones.

But while I hesitated footsteps came rushing towards us. Joyce appeared swirling the bag of remnants round her head like a tomahawk. I ducked instinctively.

"Rose sent me with these," she panted. "She thought you would be disappointed not to have them." Giving the bag a final flourish she tossed it into my waiting hands.

"Edna was just about to run back — weren't you?" mother said meaningfully.

"Oh, yes." I smiled gratefully at Joyce, mesmerised by the sight of her spectacles half-way down her perspiring nose. "Thanks, Joyce."

Joyce grinned and with a nonchalant "Ta ta," sprinted back up the lane. As luck would have it a tram was waiting at Doffcocker Inn. I slept on and off during the ride into town and again on the tram home but Gordon managed to hang on to consciousness long enough to relate the excitements and adventures of the day to father.

For me it was 'just a lick and a promise' of a wash before bed-time. It seemed adequate, but what my mother never realised was the revival of lively spirits which even a brief wash brought about. I felt I could easily have played a few games of hopscotch afterwards.

"You've washed the sleep away," I protested. But, as part of the bed-time ritual washing, along with 'Gentle Jesus' prayers, had to be observed come what may.

That summer our visits to Stoneycroft Farm were frequent. On fine Sundays, my father came along with us and we ate our tea with 40 or so hikers who made a beeline for the farm to partake of Mrs. Phillip's renowned spreads. Trestle tables inside and outside the house sagged with the weight of food. Rose brewed tea in colossal white enamel jugs. Everyone lingered, replete with food and mellowed by warm sun and good conversation, until the sun dipped below the hill and the first evening chill set the ladies searching for their cardigans. The view over Horwich and beyond was spectacular. Was that Blackpool Tower we could see in the far distance? We convinced ourselves it was.

By the time summer waned into autumn Gordon had acquired some farming skills and his health prospered, in fact we were all fatter and fitter than before. My mother's fantasies of the bucolic existence revived and tantalised her on and off. Not for one moment did she relinquish the dream even in winter, although Mrs. Phillips put the record straight more than once, painting a grim picture of snow-blocked lanes, days of isolation and water pumps so solidly frozen that getting them to function broke the fingers rather than the pump handle. In September school intervened. Only Rose's wedding drew us back briefly to Horwich that year.

When Rose married Jim the skies were overcast. A teasing wind tugged at her veil and tossed the trailing fronds of fern in her vast bouquet of roses like strands of loose hair.

71

The bouquet itself, big as a cartwheel and probably as heavy, held firm as a sheet anchor as Rose struggled up the church path on her father's arm. Still, she managed to convey an aura of radiance as the bridesmaids juggled with their king-size bouquets and adjusted the bride's veil for her glide down the aisle in her classic ivory satin dress. Joyce and the bridegroom's sister wore pink floral crêpe de chine which complemented the ivory and matched the pink roses in the bouquets. Joyce had a new pair of spectacles which managed to stay put on her nose.

Mrs. Phillips, in a beige two-piece, made by Rose, looked suitably overcome, the Phillips men, uncomfortable in dark suits and collars and ties walked stiffly and self-consciously, their hearts obviously back on the farm.

We threw our confetti as they came out of church but the wind blew it back in our faces. The sun made a brief appearance. Mother took out her hanky and blew her nose hard. She always found weddings emotional occasions. The wedding guests behaved with due decorum and the happy couple drove off to the photographer's, and then to the wedding breakfast.

As my mother and I clattered back home on the tram she told me a rhyme about wedding days.

> *Monday for health*
> *Tuesday for wealth*
> *Wednesday the best day of all*
> *Thursday for losses*
> *Friday for crosses*
> *And Saturday no luck at all.*

Rose, if I recall correctly, chose the best day of all.

CHAPTER 6

Moving on

Gordon's return to full health prompted my mother to utter a thought-provoking gem.

"Do you know," she said to Aunty Lizzie during one of their phases for sipping lemon tea in mid-afternoon, "I do believe we shall soon be sailing into calmer meadows."

For once my aunt was lost for words. She held her cup in her lap and contemplated it silently for a few moments. Then she smiled. "I'm sure you're right Maggie, but I'm darned if I know what the dickens you're talking about." And her smile spilled into such bubbly laughter her cup rattled in its saucer.

In thankfulness for his recovery, and desiring to foster any latent talent in us my mother made up her mind to purchase a piano. Her friend, Ethel Kenyon, on Tonge Moor Road had a neighbour wishing to sell an upright walnut piano with mis-matching stool. My mother had an ear for a catchy tune and sometimes sang snatches from '*The Merry Widow*', the Gilbert and Sullivan operettas, '*Maid of the Mountains*' and other popular music hall songs. Her soprano voice was light and melodious but uncontrolled, it tapered off into a squeak on the high notes. My father only sang in church.

We all went up to view the instrument. It appeared soundly constructed, and my parents agreed to buy it. The cost was £4.10s.(£4.50) — almost a week's wages. The problem of transport was solved by Mr. Riding, a near neighbour of ours who had a sturdy horse and cart. He promised to collect the piano one evening after finishing his coal round and deliver it safely to us. He arrived a few days later at our front door, with the piano roped to his well-scrubbed cart and his horse straining under the load. Luckily it was dark. My mother had been on tenterhooks before he came in case the piano's arrival would be visible to all the neighbours. Front door deliveries invited curiosity and were not encouraged so it relieved her anxiety to see the piano unloaded with no more than the pale glow of the gas lamp outside our house lighting the way in.

There was quite a bit of juggling around of the furniture before we could accommodate the new acquisition. The sofa went under the window, guaranteed to give us all stiff necks from the wicked draught if we sat on it, the square dining-table with its blue and grey plush chenille cloth took centre stage and the armchair, squeezed into the corner beside the fireplace was too far from the hearth to provide solid warmth to the feet. Still, the piano fitted well against the wall dividing the living-room and kitchen, but it proved hazardous, especially for my mother as she moved between the rooms a hundred times a day. Her hips and shins caught its sharp edges and the bruises lasted for days.

The first person to play the piano was the tuner. Even in our shameful state of ignorance we realised the need for an overhaul. Mr. Metcalfe took off the back for a thorough inspection and found the inside of the piano had provided sheltered accommodation for mice over a long period of time. Cheerfully he cleared away the debris, tightened wires, screwed knobs, tested the ivories and examined every inch with his experienced eye. To convince himself, and us, of a job well done he concluded with a wide-ranging selection of melodious tunes, pressing the loud pedal to its fullest extent. The house reverberated. We marvelled at his dexterity.

Gordon began lessons with Miss Bailey on Crompton Way. Within a matter of weeks the agony of practising scales hour after hour gave way to slightly more tuneful pieces. Another month or so and his progress led him on to adventurous melodies. Visitors listened politely as his repertoire grew to include 'In a Monastery Garden', 'Tiptoe Through the Tulips', and 'Carolina Moon'. They nodded and smiled as though they were hearing them for the first time, played by a maestro. As he mastered more complex compositions, his recitals lengthened. We had many callers to the house as my mother had a capacity for making friends and rarely a day passed without a visitor. When not a hand had been raised to knock at our door for a week my mother tumbled to the fact that the proud little pianist was to blame. With good humour and tact she persuaded Gordon to confine his mini concerts to family only. As Gordon had made such rapid strides in his mastery of the piano, it convinced my mother I ought to have lessons too. I resisted, preferring to hear my music courtesy of the wireless. Having listened to those interminable scales nothing on earth would convince me to take up the piano. Using the ever available weapon of tears I got my way. Defeated, my mother dropped the subject.

With the increasing lack of space in the house and my mother's black and blue hips from collisions with the piano corners and the fact that Gordon and I had moved to schools nearer the town, it was time for a change of residence and a good clear out of junk gathered over the years. The rag and bone man could not disguise his pleasure at the haul, declaring it was his biggest yield in a year, which spoke volumes about our piles of unconsidered trifles.

With characteristic vigour, and aided and abetted by her sisters, my mother applied herself to house-hunting. The area of choice had limits because of my father's work at

Haslam's and, in the event, it was he who found our new home in Abingdon Road. The owners of number nine, Mr. and Mrs. Cliff, intended moving into a new house being built on Crompton Way. The transaction was completed with the minimum of fuss and a cash payment of £500 secured the house. Within a fortnight the deeds and keys were in my father's possession.

Our cottage in George Barton Street was sold immediately to the Dwyers, newly-married and starting off exactly as my parents had fourteen years earlier. The pattern of life was repeating itself. Leaving friends and neighbours in the Triangle caused us a pang or two but the excitement of a move stifled any regrets.

The new house held undreamed of luxuries. A front room overlooking the green fields of Roberts' farm, a living room and a built-on kitchen. Upstairs boasted a real bathroom and Gordon and I coveted our new single bedrooms. The tiny garden at the front with minute limestone rockery and privet hedge delighted and impressed us with its beauty. The house, suitable in every way, became home for my parents for more than forty years.

My aunts exuberantly orchestrated all stages of the flitting. The occasion, regarded as a social and family affair, summoned up their blood. They made categorical pronouncements on which carpets and curtains should grace which rooms, although my mother overruled them in the end. Aunty Lizzie did her usual stint of scrubbing through the day before the move and on flitting day polished all visible areas of linoleum to a glacial sheen. Aunty Nellie hung curtains, scattered rugs in strategic places and plumped up the numerous flock cushions, lumpy and uncomfortable, on chairs and sofa. Mr. Lomax, with Albert, his five-foot two-inch assistant, who called my father 'sir' and touched his forelock each time the ladies came into view, unloaded our familiar pieces of furniture, handling them as carefully as priceless antiques. The piano created a lot of huffing and puffing as Mr. Lomax, Albert and my father heaved it along the hallway to the living room. My mother froze when she saw the chipped varnish on the front door. Otherwise it was an easy move. We had bought a three-piece suite from the Cliffs and an oak glass-fronted display cabinet. They furnished the front room. After dinner, my father feeling surplus to requirements, went to work.

As though he had come quite by chance Uncle John breezed in and demonstrated his liking for the house by pointing out the flaws. As no-one listened to a word he had to say he betook himself into the backyard and inspected the outbuildings. Then, opening the back gate, sauntered round to the front of the house and surveyed the garden, noting where improvements were required. Finding my mother unreceptive to his plans for re-organising the two square yards of soil and limestone rockery he took out his fountain pen and wrote serviceable instructions on the back of an envelope. His main concern was the hedge. To an enthusiastic and self-respecting gardener such as he, it needed radical attention. In capital letters he wrote: ARTHUR. URGENT. PRIVET HEDGE. GET IT OUT. and propped the note against the clock on the sideboard. Then as a final goodwill gesture he mended the latch on the tool shed before departing for Macclesfield.

My father, no gardener by any stretch of imagination, read the message without comment, chose to ignore it and continued for many years to trim the hedge with a second-hand pair of clippers.

When I ran in from school and flopped on the sofa I immediately felt at home. The piano caught my eye. It stood well out of bruising distance against the living-room wall. We could breathe easy.

Later in the afternoon, Uncle Arnold, wearing his undertaker's garb collected Aunty Lizzie in the hearse. And without leaving the driving seat or removing the cigarette from his mouth wound down the window and conveyed his liking for our new house by an inclination of his top hat and

77

a wilting smile. Aunty Lizzie, knowing Arnold's patience to be on a short-fuse whenever he collected her from wherever, left in a rush, setting her hat lightly on her head and fastening her coat buttons in all the wrong buttonholes.

My mother found it disconcerting to have a hearse pull up at the front gate on the day we moved in. What on earth would the neighbours make of it? There was no time to wonder. Auntie Lizzie climbed smartly in beside Uncle Arnold. Then she remembered. Leaning across Arnold she called out, "Don't forget, Maggie, I've washed everything down and polished everything up. The dusters are soaking in a bucket of Rinso under the sink."

Finding these remarks both fatuous and distateful issuing from the hearse, disapproval spread over Uncle Arnold's every feature, even his cigarette drooped at a dangerously low angle close to his chin. Suddenly starting the car, he let out the clutch so abruptly Aunty Lizzie was hurled back into her seat clutching her handbag like a lifebelt and vainly wrestling with her felt hat which lurched onto her eyebrows. We had only time to see Aunty Lizzie mouth an 'O' of startled surprise before the hearse accelerated ferociously, pinning her back against the opulent black leather upholstery, and leaving us trembling for her safety. "Well..." my mother breathed, "you'd think he was over-anxious to get her to her last resting place." Later, Uncle Sam called for Aunty Nellie. They left by more conventional transport.

By the end of that late October day the house had absorbed us as its new owners. I could hardly wait to try out the real bath. At eight o'clock I made the shock announcement that I was going to bed after my bath. My father had stoked up the fire and pulled out the damper to give plenty of hot water. In my bedroom hung cretonne curtains splashed with cabbage-sized roses which clashed disastrously with the roses on the wallpaper. Still, everything sparkled and shone, with the special brilliancy of Aunty Lizzie's exertions. The bathroom was right next door.

Intoxicated by the luxury of this new experience I made the most of it. Steam billowed forth clouding the mirror and dripping down the painted walls like rain. When I came to put on my pyjamas they were quite damp.

Bounding out of the bathroom into the bedroom I stepped on the new rag rug nestling by the bed, and Aunty Lizzie's polishing did the rest. I ended up with my right foot wedged awkwardly beneath the dressing table. Hearing the crash my mother came up to establish the worst. "Well, that's a fine start," she exclaimed irritably. "More haste less speed." Standing was out of the question and I dropped on the bed. Boiled comfrey leaves and Iodex ointment were freely applied to the rapidly swelling ankle and finally an elastic bandage. The next day I could not stand and stayed at home. I did not mind missing school; it gave me an opportunity to enjoy the new house. My mother, who had looked forward to having the house to herself was only marginally sympathetic as I hopped from room to room. The next day she encouraged me to hobble off to school.

Our second night at Abingdon Road produced a totally unanticipated event. Early in the evening my father left to attend a meeting of the Foresters and mother relaxed by the fire with the *Evening News*. I sat at the dining-table with some overdue homework and Gordon decided to play the piano. This harmonious and peaceful scene was shattered by an unexpected rapping at the window. Startled, my mother lowered the paper and Gordon's hands spread motionless above the piano keys as though he were pronouncing a benediction. My pen dripped a blot of ink on the exercise book. We sat transfixed. "Perhaps we were hearing things," my mother said unconvincingly. We returned to our pursuits. Within seconds the rapping came again with renewed force. This time my mother jumped up, switched on the kitchen light and went to the back door. Gordon and I followed.

The shaft of light from the kitchen revealed a small white faced woman with wild silvery hair, glaring angrily at us over the dividing wall grasping a clothes-prop. At first sight she looked as though she had been left out all night in bad weather. "I'm Mrs. Davies." Her strident voice congealed the blood. Hardly the welcoming overtures normally extended to new neighbours. We stared at this apparition in silence. Then mother said coldly, "Yes?" and waited for the outburst she could see brewing in Mrs. Davies's glowering expression. "I will not listen to that piano being played. It must stop. It's quite disgraceful." Stung by this unexpected outburst, mother set her face stubbornly, but stayed polite. "You will put up with it, Mrs. Davies. Gordon has to practise. He's a competent player and will not disturb you after seven o'clock in the evening. If you prefer it he can practise between five and six o'clock. But play he will." Whenever my mother met stiff opposition her head cleared and her speech became precise.

This proposal met with inaudible mutterings so my mother closed the door. Shaken by such an acrimonious exchange we returned listlessly to the living room wondering what to do next. The evening paper lay neglected on the floor and my mother sat pale and still, her hands gripping the chair arms. Gordon looked enquiringly at her. "Play for ten more minutes," she said. Simultaneously with the start of the piano the prop came at our window with the force of a battering ram. Surely the window would shatter any moment. Somehow we stuck it out and the window survived the onslaught. The piano and the prop fell into silence together.

The rest of the evening, until my father came home, passed in whispering misery. Over the playing of the piano mother made her stand on a point of principle. In our own home we were entitled to pursue a code of conduct which suited us without causing undue offence to neighbours. My father blustered about sending a solicitor's letter but mother calmed him down with uncharacteristic firmness.

As five o'clock approached the next day we jerked about like tightly-strung puppets petrified at the thought of the prop beating our window again. Gordon played the piano between five and six o'clock as mother had stipulated. The prop remained unused. The price of that small victory was that it robbed us of our appetites.

We discovered Mrs. Davies took life very seriously. She led a reclusive existence writing complaining letters to the press on all subjects she believed threatening to her well-being. She also entertained the conviction that the world trembled on the brink of the apocalypse which ruled out the need to cook, clean or wash. Far better to sit by the fire and express your opinions on paper until the catastrophic event occurred. While dismissing Mrs. Davies's view of life as incomprehensible twaddle mother nevertheless responded in her usual way, sending me round with a gift of food. Mrs. Davies, she explained, was emaciated with composing letters all day long. She feared, too, for Mrs. Davies's sanity, but how to deal with that was thankfully beyond her ken.

Over the years we came to know Mrs. Davies better, though we never crossed her threshold and she kept to her side of the backyard wall.

The initial clash with our new neighbour did nothing to detract from our enjoyment of number nine Abingdon Road but it set us thinking fondly of our neighbours in the Triangle, where whatever happened was everybody's business.

CHAPTER 7

Three sides of life

Our neighbours in the Triangle were second to none. At number 19 George Barton Street lived Mr. and Mrs. Berry both substantial figures, well rounded and fleshy cheeked. Their only child, Liza, was about 20 years old, fair, unassuming and still slim. Liza had a passion for cheap shoes, *Evening in Paris* perfume and floral cotton dresses. The Berrys lived their life entirely through the back of their house, kept themselves to themselves and troubled no one. The only regular sound was at five-thirty in the mornings when the knocker-up tapped sharply with his long pole on the Berry's bedroom window. To his credit, Mr. Berry, his cheeks quivering as he spoke, apologised for the disturbance. But my father always rose at six o'clock anyway and derived a certain satisfaction in knowing he could stay in bed for a further half hour. It was not long before my parents found they slept through the tapping of the knocker-up and resorted to using an alarm clock to waken them.

Despite their back street life, the attention of the Triangle focused on the Berrys through Liza who became engaged to Eric. Nothing dramatic in that, except that Eric worked in Africa. Speculation was rife as to how Liza, shrinking and mouse-like, had discovered a man as handsome and sophisticated as Eric.

The only time I ever saw him was when he came striding purposefully down the street on his way to visit Liza. I was sitting on the front door step reading *Chick's Own*. Even at the tender age of four I noticed Eric's bronzed good looks and fine teeth. He spotted me and smiled, "Hello, luv, how are you?" I just stared at him, too overcome to reply.

Liza's parents were quite out of their depth with Eric. A well-travelled man was an enigma to them and they would have preferred someone residing within the limits of Bolton for Liza. Africa was as remote as the moon and instead of such an exotic continent gripping their imagination, it positively crushed it. Losing Liza to Eric and to foreign parts was like a volcanic upheaval in their lives. Mother lent a sympathetic ear to Mrs. Berry's lament and she seemed only too happy to pour her troubles into it.

Liza came round reeking of *Evening in Paris* to show us her solitaire diamond ring and told us the wedding was arranged for Eric's next home leave in a year's time. Her face glowed with happiness and made her quite lovely. But twelve months gave Liza the opportunity for second thoughts. Eric returned on leave. The engagement was extended for a further year. No one questioned the decision; long engagements were considered quite appropriate. Liza dithered for three years before the wedding took place, without any apparent rejoicing. Mr. Berry's jowls fairly wobbled when he spoke about it and Mrs. Berry's strawberry colour darkened to carmine with worry over Liza's future.

My mother gave Liza half a dozen egg cups as a wedding present and then spent a sleepless night wondering if she had done the right thing. Who could say if there were hens in Africa?

When Liza had been gone almost a week and the Berry's front door appeared to be shut for evermore we were astonished to see the phenomenon of a taxi drawing up outside number 19. My mother, casting discretion aside, gaped unashamedly through the lace curtains. Out of the taxi stepped Liza wearing her brown two-piece going away suit and brown straw hat from which her marcelled hair sprouted untidily. She looked tired and crumpled. The taxi driver unloaded her luggage and Liza fumbling in her handbag to pay him, dropped the half crown on the pavement in her agitation. Then she disappeared into the house with her cases and shut the front door firmly.

Three days later Mrs. Berry gave my mother the story, flushing and paling by turns with the emotion of what she had to relate, as she dolefully confided in my mother. Liza and Eric had spent a few days in London before moving down to Southampton to embark for Africa. On the eve of their departure Eric, for some inexplicable reason, found it imperative to acquaint Liza with certain aspects of African life of which hitherto she had been in ignorance. She sobbed in disbelief when Eric explained that fish and chips, trotters and kippers were definitely not on the menu; such deprivation had never even crossed her mind. She had suffered from the sin of presumption and assumed all her favourite foods would be available.

Then there were the different customs and manners which Liza would have needed to assimilate. Also the language barrier; could Liza overcome it? Shaken to the core by Eric's seemingly casual revelations Liza said it was more than she could stomach. At least she knew and understood dirt and smoke and rain but African ways, food and weather seemed unfathomable. Even with Eric at her side, life in Africa would be intolerable and she was unprepared to try it. Leaving Eric virtually on the quayside, Liza returned home. The marriage was over. "Well... it seems he treated Liza rather shabbily," my mother said, not wholly convinced of the rights and wrongs of the affair.

The Berrys were as distressed by Liza's return as they had been at her departure. They could hardly hold up their heads for shame. The stigma of failure was like a brand on the forehead and divorce unmentionable. In Liza's case, the fact that she had separated from her husband so soon after making her wedding vows was seen as doubly damning. Nevertheless life at number 19 resumed its former pattern and, if anything, the Berrys became quieter.

These events proved too much for Mr. Berry's health. He lost weight. Several times my mother announced he had suffered an 'attack'. As she had once told me Mr. Berry had fallen arches I assumed they must in some way be responsible for his illness but when I asked about it she replied evasively that he'd had a 'seizure'. Knowing that further information would not be forthcoming I had to be content with this half-understood diagnosis but dimly realised Mr. Berry was very ill. Within a few days he had a 'relapse'. These mornings the knocker-up passed by and an eerie silence enveloped number 19. We saw Mrs. Berry wrap a piece of flannel round the door knocker, straw was laid in the street dulling the clop of horses' hooves and rattle of cartwheels on the cobblestones, visible signs that death was imminent. One morning, early, my mother noticed the Berry's curtains closed throughout the house and, realising the inevitable had happened, told Gordon and me that Mr. Berry had 'passed on'. Where to? Gordon wanted to know. Heaven, my mother said casually as she dropped Shredded Wheat into our breakfast bowls. Jim Riley's grandpa, Gordon went on, had been fortified by the rites of the Holy Mother Church when he died. God rest his soul, Jim said. So would Mr. Berry be fortified too?

Not having anticipated the simple announcement of Mr. Berry's death would bring about such depths to the conversation, my mother hesitated before answering. She poured warm milk over our cereal. Jim Riley's grandfather must have been a Roman Catholic, she explained. Roman Catholics were always fortified by the rites of the church when they died. She was not sure of Mr. Berry's persuasion, Church of England probably, so doubtless he had gone straight to heaven without the need for fortification. "Now eat up your breakfast," she urged us, determined to end this unexpected early morning debate on death. And in the rush to get ready for school we forgot all about Heaven, the rites of the Holy Church — and even poor Mr. Berry.

Mr. Berry's body lay in the front room until the day of the funeral. On that day at three o'clock in the afternoon Gordon and I stationed ourselves at a chink in the drawn bedroom curtains to gaze on a new experience. Every house in the Triangle followed custom by closing its curtains on the day of the funeral, Mrs. Norris's corner shop was shut and the blinds pulled down. As the glass-sided horse-drawn hearse and mourners' carriage moved slowly down George Barton Street every door opened and the women appeared, some in curlers, aprons and slippers, much to mother's disgust, to stand silently, with arms folded, as a mark of respect. Ritual had to be observed.

The coffin was slipped into the hearse and black curtains pulled over the glass windows. Wreaths covered the roof. The black horses, decked with black plumes, stood as silently as the crowd. The mourners, Mrs. Berry, Liza and close family, left the house in unrelieved black. The small cortège left at snail's pace and as the mourners' carriage passed our window a flash of white caught my eye. I pressed my face close to the window. Nudging Gordon out of the way, I saw Mrs. Berry's black-gloved hand shake out a white handkerchief.

Custom decreed that curtains remained closed for the rest of the day, though there was a discreet widening of the gaps once the funeral cortège was out of sight. The following morning windows were clear again, nets twitched into place, Mrs. Norris's shop bell pinged pleasantly and life resumed its normal routine.

Mrs. Berry and Liza came and went through their back door as usual. At times only a whiff of perfume betrayed Liza's presence in the backyard. Mrs. Berry stayed close to the house and when my mother came upon her in the back street one day a few weeks after the funeral, Mrs. Berry said, "I'm feeling better now," and disappeared without another word.

The Misses Rawson, two spinster sisters, inhabited the first house in George Barton Street. Both were well-built and ferociously energetic. They espoused the causes of Guiding and Brownie movements with such dedication it appeared to be their raison d'être. They both worked, but all their spare time was devoted to guiding. The practical application of guiding laws overruled all other temporal considerations. Rumour had it they slept in a ridge tent in the back bedroom using sleeping bags as bedding. Was it true, I asked, that the Rawsons never used matches but lit their fire by rubbing two sticks together and ate their food out of billy cans heated over the flames? These were all vulgar stories circulated by disreputable gossips in mother's opinion, and if ever she heard me repeating them she would...well...she would give me what for.

Occasionally, feeling concerned for their welfare, my mother sent me up to the Rawsons with half her batch of baking. I went unwillingly. Balancing the food on one hand I would stand hesitantly outside their front door debating whether to bang on it or tap gently. When I did knock smartly on one of the panels the sound thundered along the passage which led to the living-room. After an interval footsteps approached, echoing on the lino. A shock of red hair appeared as the door was flung open. This was Doris, the younger sister. Our conversation, laconic and stilted, never varied. "My mother sent this," I said handing over the paper parcel of food. Doris received it gratefully. "Ta. Oh, ta. Tell your mother, ta," she said with her eyes on the food rather than me, while I gazed in fascination at her mop of blazing hair. Then she gave the Girl Guide salute and closed the door decisively.

Every Sunday morning the two of them emerged from their front door, wearing their respective uniforms, and strode out with a determined spring in their steps on their way to church. The sleeves of their tunics bristled with badges, and sturdy silver-buckled leather belts encircled their even sturdier waists. Doris's abundant flame of hair sprung wildly from beneath her Brown Owl's hat and had to be held in place with the leather strap knotted beneath her chin. Molly had no such problems with her Eton crop, her troubles lay in her bulging calves. When she walked they rubbed together abrasively so that her seamed lisle stockings twisted like corkscrews.

The Rawson sisters conceded nothing to the dictates of fashion. When fox furs, felt cloche hats and elegant strap shoes became fashionable winter wear in the '30s, the Rawsons, eschewing all feminine adornments, strode out in Burberrys, berets and brogues. Consequently they appeared robust and ruddy-faced in comparison with their pallid fashion-conscious contemporaries. In fact, their stamina was quite terrifying and they slammed in and out of house with enviable zest as though life were one long jamboree. Mrs. Rigby observed cynically it was the only way they could keep warm.

My one encounter with the inside of their house came about when they invited me, along with five other girls, to a Beetle Drive in aid of Brownie funds. We gathered at six o'clock one dismal December evening in the gloom of their living-room, sparsely furnished with oilcloth covered table and cushionless bentwood chairs. A picture of Baden-Powell, hanging askew over the mantlepiece was the only adornment in the room; both girls gave it the three finger salute each time they passed it. The gravy brown decor added its own brand of depression and the fire —

half a dozen pieces of coal supporting each other for warmth — finally gave up the glow shortly after the first dice rattled in the shaker.

At half-time refreshments, Rich Tea biscuits and cold lemonade, chilled us to the bone. In the end, Molly had to assist me with throwing the dice, my stiffened fingers having lost their sense of direction. My beetles, drawn with increasing carelessness, looked lonely and tortured. There was small consolation in finding I had won the booby prize, half a yard of satin ribbon, and Molly had to press it into the palm of my clenched hand.

After wavering through 'Taps', the Guides' farewell song I stumped home on wooden legs. Thawing me out proved quite a struggle. The Rawsons were Spartan all right. Even mother admitted as much when she finally got my blood flowing freely again.

Somewhere between the Rawsons at number one and us at 17 lived the Bate family. Seven in all, and happy in their own way. Mrs. Bate, a fair still-pretty woman made a point of not venturing out until the streets were well-aired. The cold did not suit her. On a lovely summer evening her pleasure was to go to the doctor's surgery to have her ears syringed. The girls, Myra and Nellie, were best known to me. Myra took our Sunday School class. She read extracts from John O'Gaunt to us which we found less than riveting. However, as her quiet voice threaded through, what was to us, the incredibly tedious prose we assessed Myra's attractions, her blonde hair and creamy skin, neat appearance and fashionable strapped shoes and, above all, her long, pale-pink finger nails which were the envy of the class. Myra worked in an office and this made her particularly careful to look well-turned out at all times.

There were no flies on Nellie. Pert and lively she was the third child in the family. Although she joined us when we played in the backstreet, her talents leaned towards the dramatic and she tolerated our love of skipping, hopscotch and rounders with thinly-veiled contempt. The moment she could organise a concert her spirits lifted. Charging us a ha'penny each entrance fee to Ivy Ikin's backyard she kept us entertained by the hour and appropriated the funds: though to be fair she paid Ivy a ha'penny rental for use of the yard. Nellie had irreproachable legs which swung into action as Ivy set the gramophone in motion; she also displayed breathtaking confidence and enterprise. Her exuberant virtuosity rarely slackened and her imitations of Gracie Fields and other music hall stars held us entranced. With true professional modesty, Nellie acknowledged our applause at the end of the concert with a couple of encores and, should any of us be bold enough to exit before they finished, she regarded it as a personal insult. Once, Jean Riding, who frequently suffered the agonies of earache, tried to slip out unnoticed. Before she could unlatch the gate Nellie rewarded her boldness with an unprofessional mouthful of abuse. Jean blinked back the tears, and Nellie relented sufficiently to excuse her wrath as a sign of her highly artistic temperament. Jean forgave her, as we all did, because she was so entertaining.

Ralph and Jimmy Bate made their mark by roughing up the games, then doling out compensation in the form of segments of orange. Billy, the youngest, rarely got as far as joining in the fray; he no sooner reached the spare ground than his mother called from the shelter of the back gate, "Come in, Billy, and let me wash the sleepy dust from your eyes." Billy slunk home, red with embarrassment. When he returned, pink and clean, he immediately threw himself into a fight to prove that the humiliation of having his faced washed did nothing to detract from his toughness. Afterwards he slunk home again, bloodied and bowed, to be cleaned up and berated by his mother.

A leg wound sustained during the First World War left Mr. Bate with a limp and a pension. He worked spasmodically and paid great attention to dress, wearing dark suits and bow ties and added to the overall dapper image by using a silver-topped gentleman's cane.

Mr. Bate, popular with the children, refereed the four-a-side football matches and kept all the cricket scores in a hard-backed notebook. When any fights or tussles flared up Mr. Bate waded in with his silver-topped cane, separated the opposing factions and lashed them verbally with easy articulation which left them open-mouthed and cowed. If one of his own boys was involved, he grabbed the culprit by the ear, limped home with him and proceeded to give him another dressing-down. Nellie, clearly a chip off the old block inherited her father's agility with words.

Mrs. Clough and her daughter Ada, lived in Angle Street diagonally across from our house. A miner's widow, she was the 'wonder' who cleaned, scrubbed and polished the Congregational Church as well as taking in washing from the wealthy families of Heaton. Her hands could ladder silk stockings at a distance of two inches. Total immersion in hot water heavy with washing soda or powder for many hours a day made them as abrasive as emery-cloth. She would hold them in front of her and inspect their cracks ingrained with particles of dry shrivelled skin and swear the webs were already forming between her fingers. Working every hour God sent she still held fast to a sense of humour despite the unending toil. Ada, at 14, had left school and started as a shop assistant six days a week, spending her evenings ironing the shirts and sheets which had to be returned to Heaton the following day.

Mrs. Clough had a fondness for proverbs. I imagine she sometimes sat for a few moments rest as she mopped between the pews and picked up one of the Bibles piled up in the corners of the seats. Her favourite, oft-repeated adage, 'A good name is rather to be chosen than great riches,' kept her optimistic and proved a consolation when she felt poverty-stricken. Great riches could only ever be a fantasy for her so she really had no alternative but to go all out for the good name.

Shortly after my eighth birthday I became Mrs. Clough's errand girl. She received her wages on Friday afternoons so as soon as I came home from school I ran across the Triangle to pick up her weekly grocery list scribbled on a scrap of paper and wrapped round two half crowns. Then I raced to the Co-op on Tonge Moor Road.

As a new experience I treated it cautiously, standing hesitantly among the jumble of housewives queueing untidily for their turn to order and haggle over the fattiness of bacon and maturity of the cheese, clucking like agitated hens at the prospect of a price rise which might deplete their meagre household budgets. As I stood encompassed by these matriarchs and swamped by their shopping bags and baskets, I gradually found myself jostled to the back of the shop while they sailed forward in impenetrable ranks to the counter where they presented their lengthy lists of groceries and exchanged gossip and pleasantries as they waited for each item to be cut, sliced, weighed, bagged or wrapped.

The waiting wearied me. Within a few weeks I developed bolder tactics. Breaking ranks by ducking beneath their baskets and without so much as an 'excuse me' or 'do you mind' plunged through to the long polished wooden counter where I bobbed up and faced one of those grandees of the grocery world — the male Co-op assistant. In his long black apron, starched collar and rolled up shirt sleeves he epitomised an employee who recognised that the dividing counter gave him superior status over his customers. I discovered one of this kindly breed who, ignoring the murmurings of dissent and disapproval from the outraged women, took the crumpled shopping list and served me. Smoothing out the paper he painstakingly ticked off each item as he gathered it from shelf, counter, sack or tub, wrote down the price with his pencil fastened on an elastic at his waist and encouraged me with a smile as the list grew shorter.

Occasionally, in the early days, before I mastered Mrs. Clough's preferences, dilemmas occurred over which brand of tea or coffee she would like. Would it be Indian or Ceylon? Coffee grounds or Camp coffee? I did not know. I waited for inspiration but none came. At last some gloved finger would poke me on the shoulder and an irritable female voice urged: "Don't be such a gobbin. Say summat, else we'll be here all night. Make your mind up or buzz off."

Spurred to action, I said Ty-phoo as we had it at home; but then we sometimes had Horniman's I added. The assistant, refusing to be hustled by the women left me to make my decision before thoughtfully tapping his teeth with his pencil and reaching down a packet of Co-op tea. When all the items were assembled and counted on a sheet of strong brown paper, they were expertly wrapped into a neat parcel and tied firmly with string pulled from a ball hanging beneath the counter. Then began the totting up of prices, top to bottom first then in reverse followed by the writing of the butter-yellow 'divi' cheque making sure it passed through the carbon on the book, and finally the handing over of the change enveloped securely in the grocery list. The whole business of buying a few groceries took at least twenty minutes. The women became restive and complaining. Prudence suggested a rapid retreat but the weight and bulk of the brown paper parcel meant I had to run the gauntlet of irate housewives who had long lists of groceries, bulky baskets and an urgent desire to test the mood of the assistant should they need to put some things on 'tick'. It became clear my presence in the Co-op on Friday afternoons was regarded as an intrusion. Yet, for Mrs. Clough's sake, and the reward of a penny for my trouble, I persevered for almost two years. By the end of the first year I earned the accolade of approval from the Friday shoppers for my staying power. Complaints turned to compliments and the crowd parted like the waters of the Red Sea as soon as I entered the shop. And if ever a doubt arose about an item on Mrs. Clough's list the assistant would say cheerfully, "Don't bother yer noddle luv, I'll sort it out." I blossomed beneath this change in attitude towards me, though with hindsight I imagine they probably were glad to see me served and out of the way so they could pursue their gossip and conversation, some of which might be unsuitable for young ears.

As Mrs. Clough's errand girl I earned a penny a week. Just as I was really into the swing of Co-op day, it came to an unexpected and abrupt halt.

One summer Friday I delivered the grocery parcel to Mrs. Clough as usual. "Oh, come in." She threw open the door. She unpacked the groceries, checked the items and change from the ten shilling note (50p) she had entrusted me with and pressed a penny into my eager palm. I turned to leave. "Sit down a minute, Edna," she said, "I've news for you." We sat opposite each other across the well-scrubbed deal table. Mrs. Clough poured herself a mug of tea and a glass of lemonade for me. Breaking into a packet of Rich Tea biscuits she offered me one, taking two for herself and dunking them contentedly in her tea. She demolished them both while I debated whether to follow her example. She told me that, after years of skimping and saving she and Ada were moving from Angle Street to run an off-licence in Farnworth, where the hours would be long but the rewards satisfying. Another good thing had happened; Mrs. Clough beamed. Ada had started 'keeping company' with Bert, who had agreed to handle the shop accounts in his spare time.

Her craggy, well-lived-in face broke into a happy smile as she visualised their new life. Freed from the drudgery of scrubbing floors, mopping aisles and polishing brass and pews at the church, plus relief from the burden of washing and ironing shirts and sheets for the well-to-do, she already felt ten years younger and could leave it all without the faintest twinge of regret. She promised to let me serve behind the counter on my visits to the off-licence, which almost compensated for the loss of the Friday penny for doing her shopping.

Some two hundred souls lived in the Triangle yet we were acquainted with no more than half a dozen families. Professing an indifference to gossip my mother preferred the euphemism 'showing interest' in the neighbours. It is true she never gossiped in the street, she hadn't time, and despised women who stood with arms folded over their aprons 'gassing' the day away, but she had a natural curiosity about the lives of other people. My relationship with the families in our neighbourhood centred on the children who were available for play but first my mother assessed their suitability as my companions. They had to pass the acid test of her scrutiny. While she engaged them in conversation she ran a critical eye over their clothes, hair and, most importantly, she noted whether they kept a clean handkerchief about their person. A clean handkerchief indicated a good upbringing in my mother's book. I expect she mentally gave them marks out of ten for appearance, personality and manners, and full marks to those who could produce a clean cotton hanky.

One who passed the test with flying colours was Joan Walkden. My mother approved of Joan and her parents unreservedly and we became firm friends. Whatever Joan was allowed to do I was permitted to do likewise. An only child, she had irreproachable manners, never intruded at inconvenient times and, my mother often repeated when in Biblical mood, 'honoured her father and her mother.' Mr. and Mrs. Walkden were a sturdy couple with resolute faces and firm opinions on all aspects of life. When they spoke no-one interrupted. They knew what they were talking about. Joan inherited these characteristics and her upbringing, though strict, was not rigid.

The Walkdens lived in Starkie Road, the back of which ran parallel with the back of George Barton Street. But Starkie Road had a cut off point just beyond our back gate. The builders had abandoned it, either from lack of enthusiasm, money or ideas. The patch of spare ground, which would have held another half dozen houses, remained

96

overgrown with clumps of stunted grass and everyone used it as a short cut to the church or school while the boys played and fought on it as though it belonged to them exclusively. The houses in Starkie Road had small front gardens full of grass and lupins with the odd well-kept plot crammed with roses and marigolds. Bay windows featured front and back in Starkie Road dwellings, elevating their status. The Walkdens lived at number 11. If I went across to Joan's on Saturday evenings we sat hunched round the wireless in the hot kitchen listening to the six o'clock news and 'In Town To-night'. An evening with the Walkdens was purposeful. Once the wireless was switched off the draughts board appeared, followed by a few games of dominoes and we rounded off the evening with a game or two of rummy. At eight o'clock Mrs. Walkden called 'time'. Neither Joan nor I quibbled. Her mother's word was law. My mother approved entirely.

At all street games Joan excelled, bringing intelligence and strategy to hopscotch, whip and top and rounders. She could juggle three tennis balls at once against the backstreet wall. The rest of us tried to emulate her expertise but Joan was in a class of her own. Undeniably she had the thinking girl's approach to street games. Yet when her mother called her in, and there was no pretending we had not heard her, since she was strong-voiced and distinct in her diction, Joan immediately stopped whatever she was doing and obeyed the summons. My mother applauded such restrictive practices.

Ivy Ikin, a very different kettle of fish, also lived in Starkie Road. I never really understood Ivy. Raven-haired and black-eyed she was a round, placid dumpling of a girl with a dreamy expression. Her favourite game was hairdressing. She was inordinately proud of her perfectly formed ringlets, demonstrating how her mother rolled her hair in rags every night. Ivy knew more about hair care than reading or writing and spent hours twisting and twitching her ringlets to get them hanging evenly round her short thick neck. During one of our hairdressing sessions, Joan, testing her skill with her mother's dressmaking scissors accidentally snipped off a ringlet. Ivy flushed with anger. Quick as a flash Joan evened things up by snipping off another, pointing out to Ivy that one ringlet from either side balanced the style. We all agreed the effect was stunning. Ivy smiled and her anger evaporated as she gazed into a tiny mirror propped against the kitchen window-ledge. Joan relaxed. Still, there was the prospect of Mrs. Ikin's reaction. And when Joan spotted her, looking understandably rattled, moving determinedly up the backstreet later in the day, she fled to the shelter of the coal shed. What passed between Mrs. Ikin and Mrs. Walkden stayed a secret. But Joan did not appear in the backstreet to play for a week.

The lack of drive and ambition in Ivy carried her easily through life. When her mother called her in from play it took several shouts before she responded. The first couple of "Ivy come on in now" went unheeded. The next call developed into a great shriek, "Ivee... I..V..EE geddin or else..." Then Ivy, with a slow gathering together of herself and her belongings, ambled off home. Sometimes her mother would ask, when Ivy finally reached the back gate: "Where's Harry?" Ivy never knew. So Mrs. Ikin, who had an energetic coloratura call, with a range of at least three streets, sent the variations on 'Harry' rocketing round the district. They would have done justice to a prima donna. Sure enough Harry responded, turning into the back street twitching uncontrollably for he suffered from St. Vitus' Dance. As children we avoided him in case he lunged out inadvertently and knocked us out cold.

Joan and I felt a certain responsibility for Ivy. It was possible to lose her even in the backstreet. Her overwhelming love of food drew her towards any house which sent forth the faintest appetising whiff of cooking and, hoping she would be offered if not a meal, at least a generous taste of whatever came out of the oven, she invited herself in. My mother often found her hovering round our back door on baking days and fed her. She had reservations about Ivy though. According to my mother Ivy lived at the wrong end of the day, going to bed late and getting up late. But because of her easy-going approach to life, it proved difficult not to like her. She endured a lot of teasing from the boys as she had a speech defect and found it impossible to pronounce an 'r' "Where's Hawwy?' the boys mimicked. "How should I know," Ivy retorted placidly, picking seeds from a pomegranate with a pin, "Ah don't cawwy 'im awound, you know." And when she gave no sign of rancour they ceased to taunt her and left her to her pomegranate.

Nellie Bate was to blame for the Bug House incident. But for her graphic and dramatic rendering of the weekly film instalments, Joan and I would have been content with our occasional visits to concerts and film shows at the Victoria Hall. Nellie changed all that. The Empire Picture House, known locally as the Bug House, became a highly desirable place to visit, making the Victoria Hall seem tame by comparison.

How we prevailed upon our mothers to allow us to go, I do not know. Probably the sheer weight of our persistence wore them down. I recollect trying the direct approach and I suspect Joan did too. "Out with it," mother would say when I struggled to ask for something I knew I might not get. So I came straight to the point.

"Can I go to the Bug House on Saturday morning?"

That was a mistake. I should have said the Empire Picture House.

"No. It's a terrible place." Mother did not even lift her head from the washing-up.

"Nellie Bate says it's exciting. A new instalment every week."

"Nellie's sense of drama runs away with her sometimes. She may go to the Empire each week, but you're not going at all." My heart sank but I floundered on.

"Ivy Ikin goes."

"She's more capable of looking after herself than you. Now off you go to play and forget about the pictures."

99

Seeing my hopes fading I took a chance and said boldly. "Joan says she'll be there this Saturday."

My mother's eyebrows shot up in amazement. "I don't believe it."

"She is. She told me." Lie upon lie as I grew desperate.

The pan my mother had been scouring dropped back into the washing-up water and she dried her hands.

"I'll have a word with Mrs. Walkden," she said, anxious to confirm this unlikely story. I hung about the gate, shaking, until she returned.

"What did Mrs. Walkden say?" I asked as she crossed the back street.

"Well...," I held my breath. "Yes...Joan is going, so I suppose you can go too." Joan and I bubbled with self-congratulations on our surprising victory.

On Saturday morning Mrs. Walkden, with Joan in tow, arrived to collect me. Both were buttoned up in their winter coats. Joan wore her woolly hat and leather leggings, so my mother reached for the button hook and fastened me into mine.

Clutching our threepenny bits we set off across the cinder triangle. From the doorway my mother, nervously apprehensive about the whole venture, suddenly called, "Have you got a clean hanky, Edna?" I felt in my pocket and shook out the evidence. It gave her a measure of relief.

In a burst of generosity, Mrs. Walkden took us into Mrs. Norris's shop and indulged in two ounces of mint imperials.

"They'll keep you free from the germs which swarm through that dreadful place," she said with the authority of one who knows about these things.

It was not worth taking the tram. The Empire was no more than ten minutes walk away. We went down the broo and under the railway bridge spanning Tonge Moor Road then turned left at the bottom of Folds Road to reach the picture house. The area was not salubrious by any stretch of imagination. A raw November wind stung our cheeks and tossed our knitted scarves in our faces. But ahead lay excitement so we bore it uncomplainingly. Then it started to rain, a fine, drenching drizzle.

"Won't do you any harm," Mrs. Walkden said bracingly as she left us at the entrance.

She fixed me with a penetrating look. "Wait outside here until your mother comes to collect you both at half past eleven. Now, think on. Be careful. Do you hear?" "Yes, half past eleven." I said, anxious to go inside.

We paid our money and took our tickets. The moment we set foot inside the cinema a great tide of unrelenting noise engulfed us and stopped us in our tracks. Incredible waves of shouting, whistling and screaming rolled towards us with such force we held our hands to our ears. There appeared to be no supervision. Children ran wild, jumping up and down on the concrete floor and banging the wooden seats like gunfire. Missiles flew through the air with abandon. A free-for-all broke out in the front rows. But worse than this was the stomach-churning stench of oranges, unwashed bodies and clothes drying in the heat created by the seething mass of children. Joan tugged my hand and pointed to two empty seats by the aisle. Speech was impossible. We banged down the tip-up seats and perched on the edge. The unending flow of children up and down the aisles, the shouts and clouts, cheers and jeers and stamping feet continued unabated at the front. We sat there bemused by the utter confusion.

At last the pianist arrived accompanied by the manager, who expertly avoided a barrage of miscellaneous objects, apple cores, orange peel and paper pellets. Using a loudhailer, he appealed for silence during the performance no fighting, no throwing of food, and everyone should stay in their seat while the films were being shown. He spoke as a man without hope, resigned to what was obviously a weekly lost cause. Nellie had, of course, refrained from all reference to this part of the proceedings in her glowing accounts of the serial at the Bug House.

The pianist struck up as the manager retired. The lights went out and the film flickered jerkily into motion, upside down. Immediately the stamping, whistling and boo- ing began. The pianist played his heart out in the darkness while the film was righted. When it came on again I was dismayed to see it was a Western. Cheers rang out for the goodies, boos for the baddies and throughout, there continued the general walkabout and flying objects aimed at the screen.

I put my lips to Joan's ear.

"Shall we go home?"

"Yes," she mouthed.

But even before we had time to stand up, a passing boy pounced on Joan's hat and jerked it from her head. Then he launched himself off down the aisle, swinging the hat in the air. Terrified, Joan jumped up and made to follow him.

"Don't go down there," I screamed after her.

She turned briefly and screamed back, "I must." And within moments was lost in the dimness.

I stood in the aisle not knowing whether to follow or stay put. Discretion being the better part of valour, I stayed where I was. In the oblique light of the projector beam I watched the woolly hat's progress down the aisle and along the front seats. Joan was nowhere to be seen though I guessed she would be pursuing the twirling hat. Several hands reached out to grab the trophy as it waved aloft, but luckily the boy held on, otherwise it would have joined the barrage of missiles still being hurled in all directions. The pianist, a mere silhouette in the hazy light, valiantly pummelled the keys, unnoticed, unheard and apparently unconcerned for his safety. Just a routine performance.

The woolly hat turned into the far aisle, making steady progress towards the exit. Like the Pied Piper, the hoodlum had gathered a fantail of followers bent on mischief. I thought I caught a glimpse of Joan striving to reach the leader. If I left the exit on my side I realised I should meet the Pied Piper coming out of the other door. I would not know what to do if I met him face to face. The manager would help but where was he? Usherettes in this cinema were non-existent. They would have been trampled to death. The ticket office would be closed as there was not a continuous performance here.

Then the projector broke down. For a minute or two there was pitch darkness and bedlam. In my anxiety to get out I set off up the aisle using the end seat of each row as a guide. Bodies seemed to be hurling everywhere but by clinging to the seats I kept upright. Suddenly with a rattling crash the film sprang to life again producing a lull in the rowdy catcalls. I got my bearings — two rows to the exit. Pushing against all obstructions I soon found myself standing by the box office. There was no sign of adult life. While I debated what do to next the other exit door opened and out came the boy with Joan's hat. In daylight he appeared to be about 12 with close-cut spiky hair and an insolent face. He had the swaggering walk of a bully. With his retinue of scruffy followers, eager to witness a rousing confrontation, he faced me with a sneer.

"What's in that bag?" he demanded.

"Which bag?" I said stupidly, suddenly realising the untouched mint imperials had survived the turmoil and were still in my hand.

"Sweets," I said.

"Give 'em ter me."

"No."

"Ah sed, give 'em ter me..." His voice became menacing. I shook but clung on. It must have been fear that gave me the flash of inspiration. "You can have them if you hand over the woolly hat."

He spat on the floor, tossed the hat way over my head and lunged for the paper bag. It burst and the mints peppered the floor like hailstones. Undaunted, he got down on his knees scooping up as many as he could into his trouser pockets.

"What's all this about then?" The manager's bulky figure towered above the grovelling boy.

"Are these your sweets?" the manager said turning to me.

"Yes," I said breathlessly, "but I don't want them."

"I should think not now they're all over the floor." He tapped his foot impatiently while the Pied Piper gathered up the last of the mints. The little gang of supporters had mysteriously melted away. As the last few mints disappeared into the boy's mouth, the manager flexed his muscles. "Get up," he rasped. "I've seen the likes of you every week, coming here, not to watch the films but to cause trouble. Now clear off or I'll take you by the scruff of your neck and throw you out."

The boy straightened up, dodged the manager's swinging arm and darted back into the black hole of the cinema. Realising the futility of following, the manager handed me sixpence to buy more sweets. He regarded me with curiosity.

"Are you here all by yourself?"

"No. But I've lost my friend. That boy pinched her hat and she went off after him. I haven't seen her since." I went to pick up Joan's wet and grubby hat.

"Tell me her name."

"Joan Walkden."

"Don't worry. You stay here. I'll find her." He sounded unsure of success.

At that moment Joan tumbled through the exit door, tearful, bruised and dishevelled. Between her sniffs she said that when the film broke down she tried to rush to the exit but collided with another moving body, fell against the sharp edge of a seat and before she could regain her balance someone viciously kicked her ankles. All her troubles faded though when she spotted her hat. The consequences of going home without it were unthinkable as her mother had knitted it. She rammed it back on her head.

104

The manager ushered us to the street. "I don't know what your mothers are thinking about letting two nice girls like you come here." He was mystified and puzzled as though something improper had taken place. "If I were you I'd run home."

The rain was lashing the streets when we got outside. We ran as fast as our legs would carry us, spattering our leather leggings with mud as we ploughed through puddles and driving rain.

Full of remorse at being taken in by Nellie and expecting at the very least a good telling off we parted at our back gate. It was not yet eleven o'clock. Letting myself in as stealthily as a thief I stood, wet and miserable, on the doormat waiting to see which way the wind blew.

My mother, peeling vegetables at the sink, glanced up showing neither anger nor surprise. It was almost as though she expected me. I could not understand it. No recriminations. No "why are you home so early?" No "Look at you, wet through and muddy. What have you been up to?" I stood there shivering. "Well..." she actually smiled, "You are soon back. Let me get those wet things off. You look like something the cat's dragged in" and laughed.

To be treated like a prodigal daughter dispelled all the morning's misery, my soaking clothes and cold bones. I laughed too, happy to go along with her exceptionally benevolent mood, though I was puzzled.

The truth came out later. There had been a conspiracy. After weighing up the implications of allowing us to visit the Bug House, Mrs. Walkden, relying on her sound instincts, suggested to my mother they should give their permission. "Give them enough rope and they'll hang themselves," she said stoutly. Not without some misgivings mother agreed. As things turned out the common-sense psychology paid off handsomely.

We both went down with colds. Mrs. Walkden found a flea in Joan's bed; Joan and I shared the manager's sixpence. The whole bizarre episode became an abiding memory.

Next time I met Nellie I told her I found the Bug House awful. She laughed so much, holding her sides and wiping her eyes with the hem of her dress, I started to walk away. She ran after me and tugged at my arm. "You are a ninny," she gasped, sucking in air so she could speak. "Nobody in their right mind goes to the Bug House."

Her casualness astounded me. "But what about the serial film? All those instalments you told us about?"

"Oh that," she said airily in her normal voice, "I saw one instalment at the Regal and made up the rest."

Naïve and gullible, I had no ready answer to that. A point had been made and taken. My glance missed Nellie by about six inches when I met her after that, a trick I picked up from Aunty Lizzie who used it with great effect on anyone who displeased her, but we were friends again before long. Nellie's personality proved irresistible.

The Aspinalls in Leslie Street were outside our circle of acquaintances until Violet Hayes spotted their budgie in its cage at the front door. She delayed her errand to the shops to speak to the bird as it sat inert on its perch looking lonely and bored. Mrs. Aspinall came to the door to investigate.

"That's Billy," she said to Violet, "I'm trying to learn him to talk." Pursing her lips she leaned close to the cage. "Pretty Billy. Pretty boy. Give us a kiss Billy," she pleaded. But her efforts met with a silent, unblinking stare. She turned to Violet. "Will you try?"

Violet repeated a few feeble Pretty Boys and Pretty Billys. Responding, Billy made a noise which sounded like a cross between a chortle and a raspberry. Violet gave up. "Don't let that put you off. Come any time," Mrs. Aspinall said encouragingly. "The more people talk to Billy the sooner he'll say something."

106

The next time Violet went to say a few words to Billy she took me along for moral support. Mrs. Aspinall bubbled a welcome and sat us in front of the cage with instructions to keep saying the same phrases over and over. She was a buxom blonde, 'all peroxide' my mother said scathingly, with a light baby-high voice which developed into a whine whenever she spoke more than two sentences together. She seemed quite old to us which means she was probably all of 35 and had no children.

"Hello Billy," Violet and I crooned, "Pretty Billy. Pretty Boy." We felt we had the potential to succeed where Mrs. Aspinall failed. Our confidence soon dissolved however as Billy moved from perch to swing, looking disdainfully down his beak at us, his bright eyes showing a surprising degree of awareness and intelligence. Following Mrs. Aspinall's example, Violet put her lips to the cage and made a kissing sound. Then I tried. All to no avail. We soon realised there was no pulling the wool over Billy's bright eyes. He knew exactly what we were up to and refused utterly to co-operate. Hopping back to his perch he cracked a bit of birdseed and outstared us.

Our lips grew stiff and voices monotonous with the constant repetition. Billy's sterling quality was silence. Mrs. Aspinall served us milk and Madeira cake, requesting us not to make crumbs. The house was spotless. Shining brass horseshoes hung on either side of the fireplace and the mantlepiece held polished brass bells and crinolined ladies. A brass coal scuttle and brass fire irons sparkled on the hearth, and elaborate painted vases on lace mats flanked the Napoleon clock on the sideboard. Billy's cage rested on the cloth-draped sewing machine and caught the husks of seeds which he flicked through the bars. When I described the room to my mother she said, "Just as I pictured it, and not a crease in the cushions I suppose." I think she was nettled because we could boast only one brass plaque which she hardly ever noticed so rarely was it cleaned, and our cushions were recognisable as such only when they were plumped up to smoothness at the beginning of each day.

Out of the goodness of our hearts Violet and I fed Billy a crumb or two of our cake. He snatched them fiercely and looked for more, but Mrs. Aspinall came through from the kitchen so we ignored Billy and finished our milk. Suddenly Mrs. Aspinall said, "It's Billy's flying time now" and opening the door of his cage gave him his freedom. Neither Violet nor I were prepared for this. After flying into the kitchen he swooped round the living-room, careered above the curtains, touched down briefly on the picture rail and landed on the clock. Violet and I stood still as statues while Billy selected his next port of call. What if he landed on my head and entangled his claws in my hair or in Violet's short blonde tresses? I closed my eyes and waited. When I opened them Billy was sitting on the back of the couch, his bright beady eyes fixed on Violet. But Mrs. Aspinall, aware of our tembling terror, took pity on us and captured Billy, setting him back on his perch and fastening the cage door firmly. He regarded us balefully. I was convinced he would hold his quick return to captivity against us and next time would doubtless not only land on our heads but give us a nasty peck on the nose into the bargain. Our enthusiasm for giving Billy further speech therapy that day evaporated and after a few more Pretty Boys and Pretty Billys, Violet and I went home.

Despite the fear of having Billy flying about us, Violet and I took to calling regularly at the Aspinalls, as much for the Madeira cake and milk as teaching Billy to talk, and Mrs. Aspinall made much of us saying we were welcome any time. No amount of coaxing though could persuade the bird to utter anything comprehensible. On warm days his cage, atop a stool, stood outside the house in the hope passers-by would stop and murmur appropriate bird phrases. They did and they failed.

Mrs. Aspinall began to give up hope and her husband, who sometimes arrived home while we were there, growing tired of hearing his wife's baby-fine voice complain of Billy's inability to say even one word, ignored her recital of the budgie's latest antics with: "Oh bugger bloody Billy. Where's my tea?"

"Watch your language, Joe." Mrs. Aspinall looked apologetically towards us. Joe shrugged his shoulders. "These kiddies'll 'ave 'eard such words, and worse I reckon, afore." He grinned at us standing silently by the fireplace looking as though butter would not melt in our mouths. Mrs. Aspinall produced a bottle of Bass to calm him down, then she removed herself to the kitchen where the conspicuous clatter of pans and crockery signalled the preparations of a meal. As a tram conductor Mr. Aspinall worked shifts. His bulky figure, flat feet and downturned mouth made him unattractive and, not having children of his own, our presence irked him. He soon cottoned on to the fact that Billy's flying time unnerved Violet and me. When he felt we ought to leave he would say, as though to reassure us: "Don't worry. I'll just let Billy have a bit of a fly round." It worked unfailingly. Violet would give a thin smile. "We must go now, mustn't we?" she would say, turning to me. Mr. Aspinall had the front door open before I had time to reply.

One day when we arrived Mrs. Aspinall seemed unusually despondent. "God moves in mysterious ways," she said flatly, "and God knows there's nothing more mysterious than the way Billy's brain works." We looked suitably downcast. Billy cracked some birdseed and kept quiet. Joe's patience, Mrs. Aspinall told us, was wearing thin. What with the cost of birdseed and litter plus little extras such as a mirror for the cage and all for no reward from Billy, it just wasn't worth the bird, Joe decided. Billy's future hung in the balance. As she prepared our milk and Madeira cake we craned our necks close to the cage, glaring into Billy's unblinking eyes and hissed; "Bugger bloody Billy" over and over until we heard Mrs. Aspinall's footsteps moving acros the kitchen towards the living room when we switched to: "Hello Billy. Good boy Billy." He blinked knowingly, but no sound escaped his beak. We wilted in defeat. Mrs. Aspinall, crestfallen and dejected, seemed close to tears.

Violet and I made ourselves scarce before Joe came home. The excitement of saying 'Bugger bloody Billy' which were, of course, forbidden words exhilarated us and we ran home repeating them ever louder until we reached the danger zone of our back gates. How our mothers discovered our lapse in language we could not imagine. It never occurred to us that we might be overheard. It brought swift action. Mrs. Aspinall's was out of bounds whenever Mr. Aspinall was present. Bad language could not be tolerated. We went along one more time.

Violet left it to me to explain to Mrs. Aspinall why we should not be calling to see her and Billy again. As I uttered the offending words Billy mimicked them as clearly as if it were Joe himself speaking. Mrs. Aspinall was ecstatic. She really loved that stubborn little budgie. As a reward she opened Billy's cage and gave him extra flying time. We left the moment Joe came through the door.

Violet heard the final chapter of Billy's story from Mrs. Aspinall a few days later. Joe had laughed to think Billy had chosen his robust words as his first utterance. He found it a great joke. "Right, Bella," he said, dropping heavily into his chair, "let's be hearing Billy talk." He noticed the empty cage. "Where is that little bugger Billy?" Realisation dawned. Joe sprang to his feet.

It was a horrible moment Mrs. Aspinall told Violet. When Joe stood up he found Billy crushed to death on the cushion beneath him. He was really upset but there was nothing he could do. With true Lancashire grit he buried Billy that night in the strip of soil in the backyard. Next day they bought Billy II. He became a front runner in the speech stakes. He was so garrulous the only way the Aspinalls could shut him up while they held a conversation or listened to the wireless was by throwing a towel over his cage.

Violet and I had no interest in Billy's successor. Budgies never featured on our present lists. And the Aspinalls drifted out of our lives.

110

CHAPTER 8

A touch of class

When I started school the daily routine of Tonge Moor Infants' was almost second nature to me. Gordon had presented the case for regular attendance at school for two years before I began. "Don't think you can come home at playtime," he said with the superiority of six terms' experience, "because you can't. So there." He made it sound like a prison sentence.

Miss Sim, the Headmistress, was petite, trim and raven-haired. Her views on education held to accepted tradition. Added to this, her fastidiousness about promoting the virtues of good manners and cleanliness were second to none. She did not suffer fools gladly.

For my first day at school I wore a shantung blouse and navy box-pleat gym tunic lovingly made by mother. To my surprise Miss Sim picked me out from the morning assembly and set me on a stool in front of everyone in order to deliver an impassioned plea for the advantages of school uniform, based on my outfit. It appealed to her sense of neatness and order. But she must have realised her exhortation would fall not only on deaf ears but also an empty purses. And few mothers were as dedicated to dressmaking as mine. Still, one or two girls did respond to Miss Sim's call for the wearing of blouses and tunics, but we were embarrassingly conspicuous in school.

Miss Sim may have been impressed by my clothes but failed to be impressed with me. Despite her lack of height she had an awesome presence.

During morning prayers silence had to be absolute. One morning I dropped a glass bowl on the hall floor in the middle of prayers. The crash reverberated like an unexpected crack of thunder on a still summer night. Hauled to the stool again and reprimanded as a glaring example of clumsiness and inattention, Miss Sim confiscated the bowl without enquiring why I had it. In fact, its purpose was to hold water for our painting lesson. Now I counted it lost and suffered further rebuke from the teacher for my carelessness. "I suppose you'd better share with Elsie Walton," teacher said acidly.

One week later Miss Sim stepped trimly into the class-room. We rose to our feet as one. Holding up the offending glass bowl, she demanded to know whose it was. I raised my hand.

"Have you lost your tongue, Edna?" Miss Sim was quickly exasperated.

"No, Miss Sim." With an impatient click of her tongue, which implied, 'Stupid girl', she handed me the bowl. Miss Sim, I decided, did not like me at all. Worse was to come.

Towards the end of the summer term, Miss Sim took it into her head to observe a practice session of our dancing display which would be performed in the final week. Immediately I noticed her standing by the piano my concentration dissolved and my legs began to discover a life of their own. I got out of step, ruining the whole dance sequence. Miss Sim's acute sense of rhythm was inflamed by my inability to get back on the correct foot. Fortunately the end of the lesson was in sight and all my thoughts were set on the bell ringing to signal a merciful release. That day it failed to ring which threw me into even more confusion and I tripped over the heel of the girl in front. Miss Sim, incensed, could barely contain herself.

112

Although not in charge of the class, she exercised her authority by rapping sharply on the piano lid with an errant ruler she discovered lurking under a pile of music sheets. The piano ceased abruptly. Surprised by the sudden absence of sound we all came to an unprepared halt, lurching into each other like a line of toppling dominoes. Miss Sim's sharp eyes rested on me disdainfully.

"Take Edna out of the circle. At once." Her dark eyes glittered with annoyance.

Once excluded from the ring of dancers I was left to stand ignominiously on the sidelines among the pile of discarded shoes and smelly socks, convinced I was the only girl in my class and possibily the whole school who did not know her left foot from her right. There and then my deeply cherished dreams of a career as a prima ballerina faded for ever.

Another couple of raps on the piano lid and the music re-commenced con brio. The circle re-formed. Dancing resumed.

"Ah," Miss Sim said, her face relaxing into a smile, "that is much better." She tapped her tiny, neat foot jauntily. "Yes, much better."

Next morning Miss Sim sent for me. Sick with apprehension I entered her room. She regarded me in silence for a minute or two then came straight to the point. Unless I could master the co-ordination of my limbs and keep in step with the other girls she would have to impose a ban on my participation in the dancing display.

"Do you understand?" she said, her voice devoid of sympathy. Oh, absolutely. Miss Sim was a stickler for just retribution and I found the intensity of her manner quite fearsome, but she seemed unaware of it.

"Yes, Miss Sim." It came out in a whisper.

Inexplicably instead of being demoralised by the ultimatum I found it a challenge, for I loved dancing. I told my troubles to my mother. She came up trumps. We had a rickety wind-up gramophone, somebody's throw-out, and two records of Viennese waltzes. Each day for a week when I came home from school, mother laboriously wound up the gramophone, set the needle on the edge of the record and off we went, left foot first to the tinny, uneven music. Without fail, the needle got stuck in a groove or slid along a scratch. We began again. Right foot first this time. My utter stupidity over left and right tossed my mother between hysterical laughter and impatient despair. But miraculously, by the end of the week, I showed signs of improvement. Now when the music started we set off together round the living room table, progressed to the kitchen, finally moving into the back yard and I had not missed a step.

But mother's problem, apart from me, was stamina. At the end of the week, the dedication and effort took their toll, and declaring herself 'Done in' she flopped into the easy chair. She could do no more for me. Now I was on my own. The overworked gramophone also packed up. Without my mother and the music, learning left from right was not fun anymore.

She was still in the chair when father came home from work. Not a man to show excessive emotion, his concern that no tea had been prepared, a crisis by his standards, shocked him into enquiring after my mother's health. The unaccustomed solicitude roused her. She tottered into the kitchen and put the kettle on.

"What's for tea?" my father called from the living room. He was half-heartedly watching my demonstration of neat footwork but failed to show enthusiasm. His thoughts were dominated by hunger pangs.

"A bit of thick seam."

My father visibly brightened. He was very partial to tripe. We always ate it raw, well seasoned with salt and pepper and liberally sprinkled with vinegar.

He actually turned to me and said, "Well done," though I wasn't doing anything at the time. It was a weight off his mind knowing tea would soon be on the table.

114

Over tea my mother told him the gramophone had packed in. Later he dismantled it, said it was 'out of flunter' and beyond repair. Anyway, he said, he was thinking of buying a wireless. They were so much better than a gramophone. We all felt cheerful. Mother laughed a lot to think we should soon be able to boast we had a wireless in our house.

At the final rehearsal of the dance display the teacher permitted me to join in. After a couple of false starts, which threw the other girls into disarray, I got it right. Miss Sim appeared. Her presence caused a tremor of uncertainty. I set off on the wrong foot. Somehow she curbed her irritation and even commended my progress as I fell quickly into step. Against her better judgment, I believe, she conceded that I could consider myself a member of the dancing team. I skipped home left, right; left, right; bursting with the exciting news.

The day of the dancing display promised fair. Unfortunately, I did not. I wakened hot and feverish, my body covered in a bright red rash. Dr. Douglas was summoned. German measles was diagnosed. Miss Sim must have thanked her lucky stars or divine providence at my sudden indisposition. A precisely worded message, via Joan Walkden, arrived from Miss Sim. Under no circumstances must I return to school until I was completely recovered.

Despite these early rifts I attended school willingly, but it came as a shock to discover not everybody liked me.

After three years in the Infants, it was time to move on to Junior School. Before Miss Sim dismissed us forever there was a final celebration of our varied abilities. The whole class had to write a story or poem or recite one from memory, sing a song, dance, or in some way entertain the rest of the school, singly or in unison. For the painfully shy the teacher rehearsed a little choir. Two or three others grouped together to recite. My offering, a poem about a poppy, was accepted as of sufficient merit for me to declaim it to the uncritical school audience. Although I did not steal the show my breathless rendering of the sad little verse was well received. To my amazement I noticed Miss Sim applauding. Flushed with the glory of the moment I returned to my place on the hall floor. Violet Hayes, grinning maliciously, was waiting. She leaned forward from the row behind and hissed in my ear. "Did you know your knickers were showing — all the time?"

The year I moved up to the Junior School was the year Gordon developed T.B. His absences from school were so frequent that he was unable to guide me through the intricacies of long multiplication and money sums. Adding and subtracting pounds, shillings and pence became an ever-deepening mystery, but in mental arithmetic I found a challenge. I loved its rapid question and answer technique soon over and done with unlike the complexities of long division and adding up sums which reached the realms of thousands and covered a lot of paper. Miss Lord, tall and stately, wondrously mild and patient, bestowed praise and encouragement with a smile though she was not beyond criticising idleness and inattention. Leaving her class and moving up to Standard III and Miss Olive caused me a pang of sorrow.

Junior School had a more varied curriculum. The school band was just one supplementary activity, sports another, and the subject of sewing was introduced by Miss Olive. No one envied her the painful task of ensuring each girl produced a hand-made garment by the end of the school year. Some made raglan-sleeved blouses. They were the fortunate ones. My garment, a pair of bilious yellow cotton bloomers, was so hideous and so roomy that Elsie Walton and I together could easily have fitted into one leg. It provided a rich source of good-natured laughter when mother came to view the sewing on display at the end of summer term. My crafted creation lay spread-eagled on the end of a long trestle table, pinned to it like a butterfly, along with other handwork, with my name fastened on the left leg. All the cutting out and sewing had been done at school so

116

that the finished product held an element of surprise. It had been sewn by my careless hands amid much toil and sweat and a few tears. Like all mothers, mine was prepared to be delighted and impressed. We moved along the trestle table, mother taking time to admire Elsie's blue Magyar blouse and Audrey Dearden's rosy pink knickers, neatly stitched with the French seam immaculately executed. Finally we arrived at my bilious bloomers. Mother's face was a study. It was difficult to decide whether she was pleasantly surprised or completely mystified. Her mouth twitched, she tried to stifle a burp of amusement by turning it into a cough, then hurriedly scrabbled in her bag for her handkerchief before finally dissolving into uncontrollable laughter. I knew her mirth was not at my expense but at the ludicrous baggy bloomers in their sickly yellow colour. My initial reaction was, should I laugh or cry, until I noticed Elsie and her mother laughing, also Barbara and Mrs. Rushton and the rest of the mothers and daughters. Everybody found my mother's hilarity infectious so I had no alternative but to join in. Even Miss Olive laughed which made it a special event. Those blooming big bloomers gave years of service as window dusters.

Progress through Junior School was less eventful for me than the Infants. Mr. Cook, the headmaster, was a remote figure who appeared at morning assembly, administered discipline by lecture and cane and gave a short homily in his gloomy eyrie above the front entrance to the school to those who were about to leave the establishment for the final phase of their education. He was a florid man with thinning, brown hair and much given to tweeds and tobacco. We saw little of him but rumour had it he was 'sweet' on Miss Twisse, the senior teacher. She was tall, bespectacled and benign, with pale golden hair bound into a bun like a ring of Cumberland sausage. She made learning fun because of her delightful sense of humour. Miss Twisse with dubious admiration likened us to 'little bees'. How or where the rumour about Mr. Cook and Miss Twisse started I have no idea but it provided whispered excitements among the coat pegs in the cloakrooms.

The most frequent interruption of school routine came from the nurse who, with the aid of a steel comb repeatedly immersed in carbolic, regularly searched our heads for signs of lice and nits. To be infected by other children's headlice was one of the major hazards of school life. We dreaded the arrival of the 'nit nurse' in case we were contaminated, as most of us were at some time. It was virtually impossible to escape at least one infestation and I remember my feeling of horror when the nurse produced a fat living head louse on the steel comb which had been drawn through my short hair. I took home a note and mother was upset but not dismayed. With the fine tooth comb and special shampoo, a nightly ritual was established which was effective within a week.

The other untimely diversion in our daily round was the arrival of the dentist. After my ninth birthday, he came to inspect our teeth. Mine, it appeared, needed 'treatment'. Again I took home a note. Mother was instructed to take me to the school clinic in Bolton the following week. 'No food or drink for six hours prior to the appointment' appeared on the note in large black letters. I went as a lamb to the slaughter. I was surprisingly unafraid, needed no bribery and did exactly as I was told which was: 'Blow away the nasty smell as hard as you can. That's right. Big breaths and b – l – o – w' as the large rubber mask was clamped over my nose and mouth and the ether seeped into my lungs.

When I regained consciousness the nurse was walking me up and down in a cloakroom urging me to be sick. I am not sure that I obliged, but I had to clear my system of the ether somehow. I remember when she left me to stand alone for a few minutes, I swayed drunkenly over the wash basin. Eleven of my teeth had needed 'attention'. My mother did not demur or react with shock at my bloodied state. And it would certainly never have occurred to

Standard I, Tonge Moor Junior School, 1933. Edna, is seated extreme right on the back row, with Violet Hayes, the budgie tutor, next to her. Barbara Rushton, the 1930 bride, is extreme left on the second row from the front.

Standard IIa, Tonge Moor Junior School, 1933. A tie-less Gordon sits cross-legged on the front row next to the boy holding the chalked slate. Clifford Ainscough, happy recipient of Gordon's generous gift, is second from the left on the second front row.

her to complain about the massacre of my teeth. She showed concern, of course, kept me home from school for a day, fed me on 'pobs', bread soaked in warm, sweet milk, until my gums had healed. Rather she accepted these extractions as a new, sophisticated technique, since her experience of dentists in her youth was that having an extraction consisted of a stunning blow on the head and the teeth yanked out while the patient was still concussed from the thwack of the wooden mallet.

Apart from these two hiccups in school life we continued to learn the 'three-Rs' to the best of our mixed abilities and life moved on pleasantly enough with little to vex us apart from petty feuds among ourselves in the playground and boastings about the number of gold stars gathered in our exercise books.

The time came to move on. Elsie Walton and John Kemp won scholarships to Bolton School. My new destination was to Bolton Municipal Secondary School, known irreverently and affectionately as the 'Muni'. On our final day at Tonge Moor School, Mr. Cook summoned all school leavers to his study. As we shuffled uneasily in the cramped space, I settled my gaze on Mr. Cook's face, and became fascinated by the intricate pattern of blue veins clustering high on his cheeks. He maintained an air of intellect which kept us in fear of him. No tears were shed at our final meeting with Mr. Cook. His valedictory banalities fell with the thud of old fruit. Having been repeated so often over the years they were totally devoid of freshness and substance. Mr. Cook held out his fleshy hand and allowed us to shake it. "Good luck," he repeated mechanically to each of us. The relief at being dismissed made me impatient. On the way down the dark narrow staircase, I missed a step and catapulted into the school hall. In the general excitement of leaving junior school behind us for ever, no one even noticed my undignified exit.

Bolton Municipal Secondary School, an unlovely sturdy building of blackened brick in Great Moor Street, was

119

a co-ed school. The school was on the same side as Moyle's dress shop. Sometimes we would gaze at the modish gowns and wonder if, when we grew up, we should be able to afford such expensive clothes. We were more attracted to Gregory and Porritt's on the other side of the street which was similar to Woolworth's though it did not pursue Woolworth's policy of 'Nothing over sixpence'. And further up from G & P the Turkish Baths forever held its mysteries, for none of us ever discovered the rituals conducted behind its uninspiring façade.

Mr. Grundy and Miss Hoyle, joint heads of the establishment organised us superbly and disciplined us with prudent firmness. Life at secondary school was diverse and interesting. New subjects, new friends and new activities captured my interest so much that by the end of my first year I ran into trouble not only academically but with the Headmistress. My partner in crime was Ethel Ainscow, a new friend, who would also soon become a near neighbour though neither of us knew it at the time. One hot day towards the end of summer term, we decided to walk home from school. Our bus fare could be spent on ice cream. The exercise of walking would be beneficial. We were in high spirits. Tipping our panama hats to the back of our heads like sombreros with the elastic round our throats we licked our cornets, swung our satchels nonchalantly at each other with total disregard for other pedestrians and spent a great deal of time convulsed with laughter over nothing. It all seemed such harmless fun until the next morning.

School Assembly passed with its customary hymn, prayer and reading followed by the day's announcements. Miss Hoyle, a supreme champion in the Headmistresses' League, presented a redoubtable figure with an appropriate degree of gravitas. She eyed us from the lectern like an intrepid Boadicea. Of majestic build, with horn-rimmed specs and rich nut-brown hair drawn into a bun, she looked as though she could have led us to victory in any battle of life. She exuded scholarly intelligence and self-control, and her ability to invest a single word with profound meaning made me think she could have dramatised the dictionary. We respected her from afar. She was not the sort of person who would clasp any of us to her bosom should we succumb to an identity crisis. Emotional outbursts were emphatically discouraged.

Once the daily announcements were made, we waited to be dismissed. Instead, Miss Hoyle beamed her regal glance over the assembly. Her mood was imperative.

"It has been brought to my attention," she said grimly, "by a member of staff, that two third form gals behaved with flagrant disregard for school rules and good manners on their way home from school yesterday."

Her gaze ranged over the ranks of silent, uneasy pupils.

"These gals were..." she paused, searching for the mot juste, "...disporting themselves in such a manner, that a member of staff was compelled to step into the gutter...yes, the gutter, in order to proceed on her way. Furthermore, they were consuming ice cream in the street. This is absolutely forbidden. The culprits need not be named, they will have identified themselves from my description." The hushed school assembly waited. Miss Hoyle smiled with stinging satisfaction. "These gals will report to me at morning break."

Unsure of Ethel's position in the school hall, I dared not look for her, but kept my eyes fixed straight ahead, feeling my face blazing like the setting sun. Break-time took an eternity to arrive. As soon as the bell rang, I pushed through the surge of bodies charging purposefully towards the playground and made my way to Miss Hoyle's study. Ethel, already there, signalled to me to knock on the door. I tapped gently. Silence. I dithered, my courage dwindling.

"Oh, let me," Ethel said impatiently and gave three smart raps on the heavy oak door. There was silence for the space of half a minute. Then we heard a resounding, "Come in."

For quite some time we stood before Miss Hoyle's desk, waiting for her to acknowledge our presence. She sat, head bent, writing industriously. Finally she screwed the top on to her pen, laid it on the desk, looked up and nodded vaguely as though reminding herself of the reason for our presence. I felt like a shrimp facing a killer whale.

Miss Hoyle came straight to the point.

"Is there anything you wish to say in mitigation of your disgraceful behaviour?"

'Mitigation', what on earth did it mean? I glanced at Ethel. "It was a hot day, Miss Hoyle," she said, "and we needed to cool off." It sounded frivolous.

"Don't make excuses, Ethel," Miss Hoyle snapped, "it is both vulgar and degrading." She eyed us disapprovingly. "You do admit your behaviour sullied the school's image, do you not?"

Completely intimidated we stood without answering.

"Well, speak up, both of you."

"Yes, Miss Hoyle," we chorused.

She picked up her fountain pen, supporting it with the tips of her forefingers as though measuring the extent of our punishment.

An oppresive silence descended. Miss Hoyle seemed to have lapsed into a state of unrelenting detachment. I shifted my weight from one foot to the other, awaiting the verdict. Suddenly we heard a tap at the door. "Come in." A smile of pure pleasure lit Miss Hoyle's face as a maid entered carrying a tray of coffee and newly-baked jam tarts, direct from the school kitchen. "Just leave it there, Doris." She indicated the corner of her desk with her pen. "Thank you."

The aroma of freshly made coffee assailed our nostrils, reminding us that break-time was rapidly disappearing. Miss Hoyle, darting a glance at the plate of jam tarts, accelerated the interview. Using her marvellous aptitude for discharging an unexpected question with the speed of a rocket, she said, "What is the school motto?"

Ethel rallied first. "Per ardua ad astra."

"Through work to the stars," I said, determined to put a word in.

122

Miss Hoyle adjusted her spectacles and moved her gaze to me. "Quite," she said with finality. "Then you can each write an essay in detention this afternoon on the value of our school motto. Plus...a letter of apology to Miss Pearce for the distress you caused her." She looked for some reaction. We gave none. "And let me make it crystal clear, any further instance of such irresponsible behaviour in public," she stopped and let the silence speak before continuing, "will not be tolerated lightly." Her brown eyes gleamed. The pot of coffee and jam tarts were a tantalising incentive to dismiss us. "Is that understood?"

"Yes, Miss Hoyle."

"Then you may go."

We heard the coffee being poured even before we reached the study door.

The incident subdued us — for about a week. Then, feeling purged of our misdemeanour we ignored Miss Hoyle's command and bought another ice cream. This time, however, we wore our panama hats at the correct angle, walked on the pavement with measured steps and licked our ice creams surreptitiously. My conscience refused to let me enjoy it. Turning to Ethel, I asked, "Don't you feel guilty?"

Ethel laughed. She possessed an enviable element of healthy disregard towards certain rules and authority which, in her estimation, were pettily restrictive.

"Certainly not, you idiotic gal," she said, imitating perfectly Miss Hoyle's imperious tones, "I feel grand."

And she finished her cornet with a flourish.

───────────────

Taking home my end of year report, my feelings defied definition. Disappointing exam results dampened my curiosity about the teachers' comments and particularly my form-master's remarks. Mr. Skuse had written:

'I expected something better than this. Early promise has not been sustained.'

My father looked at me with an unsympathetic eye when he read the report. I must have looked downcast because he did not reproach me, though neither did he treat it lightly. He simply said: "We must do something about this," and set about, in his own way, remedying certain omissions in my education.

To begin with, he bought Arthur Mee's *'Children's Encyclopaedia'* and the complete set of Dickens' works, on offer through the *News Chronicle*. While this book-buying mood was on him, my mother, seeing an advertisement for *'Home of To-day'* a guide to the modern household, persuaded him to send for that too. It turned out to be a most interesting book giving, amongst other things, detailed instructions on how to handle the servants and the best methods of bottling and preserving the fruits from the garden. "So necessary for our way of life," mother laughed.

My father's next ploy was a dedicated attempt to teach me some local history. Saturday afternoons were spent visiting various places which held some historical connection. We started with the Market Cross in Deansgate where the seventh Earl of Derby was beheaded on October 15th ,1651. Although my father was a man of few words his surprisingly graphic re-construction of this gory event put me clearly in the picture. A few yards from the Market Cross stands 'The Man and Scythe' where the Earl of Derby is reputed to have spent his last night before the execution. This ancient hostelry with its black and white timbered frontage was out of bounds for me because it sold intoxicating liquor but I peered through its tiny leaded windows and saw nothing of interest, only a crowded room of men, drinking, smoking and talking.

Nearer to home, at Firwood, we walked one Saturday to view Samuel Crompton's birthplace. As someone occupied it our imagination had to do the rest. But then, on to Hall i'th' Wood where Crompton invented his spinning mule. It was a public museum so we prowled through its rooms, creaked up the narrow wooden stairs and tried out various chairs, rocked the smooth-as-satin wooden cradle and inspected the organ which Crompton himself built. The spinning mule stood in all its fascinating splendour, the crowning glory of Crompton's career, but its complexity was bewildering, and I was much more taken with the array of kitchen utensils and great iron cooking pots. To round off our acquaintance with Samuel Crompton my father took me to see the handsome statue of him in Nelson Square.

Moving farther afield we took to roving over Belmont Moors, stopping at strategic points to gaze at Bolton in the distance, fuming in the hollow. My father explained that the name Bolton derived from 'Bowl Town' because of its geographical position, a town in a hollow amongst the moors. Out of the forest of mill and domestic chimneys Bolton Town Hall, black but beautiful, stood splendid and enduring; a magnificent landmark, clearly definable through the misty grey haze, and one of which Boltonians were extremely proud. The grime and soot beneath the wreaths of billowing smoke were invisible, of course, and when we were down there in the midst of it we hardly ever noticed it, even though it afflicted us daily like a plague.

One Saturday we made our way to Winter Hill. My father, determined I should see Scotsman's Stump, approached it from Belmont. The Stump turned out to be a cast iron pillar, erected in 1912 as a memorial to George Henderson, a travelling packhorseman from Annan, Dumfriesshire. According to the inscription on the pillar he was *'barbarously murdered on Rivington Moor, at noonday, November 9th 1838, in the twentieth year of his age.'*

My father knew some facts of the case. A collier, James Whittle, was charged with murder, but the case was dismissed when the jury found there was insufficient evidence to convict. Although locals believed robbery to be the motive for the crime, no money had been taken from

Henderson. There my father's knowledge of the event teasingly petered out. I thought about poor George Henderson for weeks.

Our final excursion took us to Turton Tower and Watling Street where we walked on this Roman Road to satisfy the desire for authenticity and to say we had trod where Roman feet had marched. My father was never happier than when he was walking and when we arrived home after our Watling Street outing my legs felt like lead. I often complained to my father about aching limbs and feet but he tended to disregard such complaints as a sign of weakness in one so young. He thought nothing of totting up 20 miles in the course of a Saturday walk. But mother declared I was 'fit for nothing' after this particular foray and so concluded our local history lessons.

With surprising meekness, I thought, my father abandoned plans to take me to Smithills Hall and Sixty Three Steps at Barrow Bridge. "Some other time," he said consolingly. His Saturday afternoons could now be devoted to cricket matches, following the fortunes of the local team. Gordon accompanied him and they talked cricket on and off from one Saturday to another.

During the school holidays, my mother took me in hand. In a last ditch attempt to teach me to sew she started me off with a simple task — unpicking the hem of a dress so that it could be lengthened. Handing me the dress and the neatest pair of pointed silver scissors and believing I could not go wrong she left me and disappeared into the kitchen. I worked slowly and conscientiously. The stitches, incredibly tiny and fine, took for ever to undo. At last, mother came in to see why I took so long to complete such a straightforward exercise.

"Just finished," I said, weary but pleased to see the end of it. My mother took the dress from me. When the bodice detached itself from the skirt, we both knew I was beyond redemption. I had snipped the last stitch of my mother's patience. From then on sewing remained a taboo subject.

With a struggle I mastered knitting, but at the first dropped stitch laid it aside and took to reading. Joan started to call on Saturdays and the two of us would sit with the encyclopaedias, passing the hours in endless fascination, while my mother sorted out the gaping holes in my kettle holders.

Returning to school in September for my second year I was relegated to the 'B' stream on the strength of my poor school report and exam results. However, my ambitions for the future remained intact — to strive to the uttermost for a place in the first hockey and netball teams. My father had done his best. He would have done more if my mother had not put her spoke in and decided I had no stamina for all this traipsing over the moors. And mother always knew best.

CHAPTER 9

Spring

The seasons shaped our lives. Each held at least one special date which kept us on our toes in excited anticipation and around which the remainder of that particular equinox revolved.

Not surprisingly spring never meant drifts of daffodils to us or the burgeoning of leaf and blossom. The first snowdrop or crocus did not send us into ecstasies of pleasure — because we rarely spotted them. And buying cut flowers was a luxury beyond my mother's purse. Our first contact with spring flowers would be if we took the bus to Bromley Cross and walked through the Jumbles where bluebells lay in great pools amongst the trees. Sometimes we discovered a profusion of wild flowers as we rambled round Seven Acres where the meadows provided rich pickings for a jam jar full of colour.

But these delights had to be deferred until after the ritual spring clean. No self-respecting housewife would dream of allowing this annual diversion to pass by as though it did not exist. Reputations were at stake. Such a time-honoured custom was almost mandatory. There was no escape. When rolls of paraffined yellow dusters, special stiff brushes and the Ewbank took up residence in the living-room we recognised them as positive proof that the cleaning crusade which would lead us into spring was about to begin. Spring cleaning in our house consisted of three distinct phases. Taking down, lifting up and clearing out. The house was in uproar for days. My father endured the chaos with conspicuous fortitude. He was inconvenienced but no words of complaint were uttered and outwardly he appeared as usual, though hardly brimming with goodwill. Seeking sanctuary in the shed, he worked wonders on the pile of repair jobs mother had unearthed during the grand clear out.

My mother hardly ever sang. However, in the first flush of enthusiasm and zest for ripping the house apart, we were treated to snatches from 'Maid of the Mountains' and snippets of music-hall songs as she carefully wrapped her dusters over the long soft brush and trawled them across the ceilings in search of lurking cobwebs. Success could be measured by the degree of blackness when the dusters were removed, the dirtier they were the greater the triumph of the exercise. And the two quart can, foaming with hot Rinso suds, stood ready to receive the victorious dusters.

Each household knew its territorial rights for the position of washing lines. On breezy days the back street presented an almost impenetrable barrier of linen and blankets drying sootily in the wind. Our curtains having been possed and washed and mangled, flapped contentedly against our next door neighbour's bedspreads.

"Did you notice, Arthur," my mother would say with satisfaction, "how everybody's pegging out? It's such a good day for it."

My father with a sly smile and wink at Gordon and me, deliberately chose to misinterpret her meaning of 'pegging out', knowing it would amuse us.

"No, I can't say I came across any bodies littering the street as I came home." We responded with giggles. But mother, clicking her tongue impatiently would say shortly, "You know very well what I mean." This subdued us. The middle of spring cleaning week was not prime time for jokey quips.

130

Carpets were lifted and Gordon and I took it in turns to wield the wicker carpet beater, flogging the Axminster to death, burning off our excess energy and relieving the carpets of their burden of dust and grit at the same time. Gordon's beatings reached an effective climax when he pretended Fred Smethurst, a perpetual thorn in his flesh, was embedded in the carpet. These boisterous batterings smothered him in choking clouds of dust, sent me diving for cover but proved an excellent method for diverting Gordon's aggression away from Fred Smethurst himself. The carpet soon looked like new again. My mother declared herself well pleased with the way we were coming to grips with the war on dirt.

After a week or more of this violent and unremitting activity, when every window gleamed, steps front and back scrubbed and donkey-stoned to pristine condition, as though this did not occur each week in the normal run of routine, furniture rubbed to a sheen that dazzled the eye, and everything that could be washed had the full treatment, the house could only be described as squeaky clean. The annual 'bottoming' process had been done again. Yet, even before the yellow dusters had time to dry, specks of soot and dust were gently lodging in unseen nooks and crannies and laying the foundations for the following year's spring spectacular.

As the house blossomed into spotless beauty those early tuneful melodies faded into a monotonous hum of desperation which indicated THE END for spring cleaning. Mother took to visiting the Market Hall for some cheap and cheerful ornament or trinket as a personal survival reward. Then she would hide it in the bottom of the wardrobe until she felt strong enough to justify the extravagance to my father. But he, only too thankful to have the house in order again gave these knick-knacks his smiling seal of approval, saying in his usual laconic way; "Yes. Very nice." And never queried the cost. I loved to go with her on these excursions. If I judged her mood correctly she would let me buy a little red notebook and coloured pencil from Woolworth's before making the rounds of the stalls in the covered market. The

131

market was an Alladdin's cave with its variety of stalls, bustle and brilliance. But first we had to run the gauntlet of the First World War survivors who sat, limbless, on the steps leading into the market from Bridge Street. Crutches were prominently displayed at their sides, often jutting out sufficiently to trip up the unwary who failed to drop a penny into the proffered flat cap. Mother tended to rush me past them, looking straight ahead.

"Why can't I give them a penny, mother?"

"Charity begins at home," she said through tight lips. "Anyway, Mrs. Boardman says some of them have their supposed missing limbs strapped to their bodies." Uncharacteristically, my mother failed to find any humour in this malpractice and was really quite scathing about it. Events proved her misgivings to be well-founded.

One day I determined at all costs to drop a penny into one of the flat caps. As we mounted the steps into the market I fell slightly behind. An opportunity presented itself. There was no one else around. But mother, intuitively aware of my sluggishness turned as I opened my fist to drop the coin and grabbing my hand, marched me on. The flat cap remained empty. Before we had moved more than a few steps, mother felt a firm poke in her back. She spun round in astonishment to see the one-armed beggar tidily replacing his neighbour's crutch on the steps with both hands. Never one for confrontation, mother nevertheless exclaimed with righteous indignation, "Well, I never! Well, I absolutely never!" Unabashed, her assailant resumed his hang-dog expression and one-armed stance, with half his jacket sleeve hanging distressingly empty. After this revealing episode I lost some of my gullibility and my charitable spirit shrivelled somewhat. On future shopping trips we always entered the Market Hall from Knowsley Street.

As our final stop in the market before catching the tram home we spent a little time in the tiny wine shop across from Bailey's china and crockery stall. Here we sat, enclosed by half curtained windows, mother discreetly sipping sherry and I, feeling very grown up, delicately drinking a Vimto. This proved to be the highlight of any visit to the market hall and reversed the decline which threatened to overcome my mother following the annual bout of spring cleaning. At home she sustained herself with Wincarnis wine — one sherry glassful taken mid-morning with a dry cream cracker. While mother administered this not unpleasant self-prescribed tonic, she also set her mind to cleansing my internal system. It was her firm belief that fluctuations in the composition of the blood occurred with the onset of spring, causing heat spots, lassitude and uncertain moods. For Gordon and me regular doses of brimstone and treacle, the inevitable Syrup of Figs and fresh orange juice, restored internal equilibrium and removed impurities from our blood streams.

The final remedy for spring upheavals lay in a short visit to Blackpool, Bispham or Cleveleys. This holiday brought the high point of our Easter school break, our first visit of the year to the Fylde coast. Aunty Nellie and Winifred invariably joined us. Father and Uncle Sam came for the weekend, returning home on Easter Monday ready for work the following day. We continued to benefit from the bracing air until the end of the week. We stayed in digs, comfortable and cheap and every fine day, after breakfast, we made our way to the beach or promenade. The sunken gardens at Cleveleys provided a windbreak. Here mother and Aunty Nellie would sit and gossip, crochet or knit, while Gordon rode his hired bicycle and Winifred and I organised our own games. The memory of one holiday lingers on.

It was a morning of bright sunshine but the cold wind drove us to seek shelter in the sunken gardens. It was the fourth day of our holiday. Mother and Aunty Nellie, deep in coversation, left us to our own devices, which happened to be skipping that day. Gordon cycled round the promenade shelters, where hardy holiday makers, their cheeks and hands often the colour of wild violets, and doubtless their knees and feet too, suffered the cutting wind stoically in the interests of health and getting their money's worth of sea air. Gordon often displayed his skill at cycling without hands on the bike, hoping to impress anyone willing to notice. On this particular morning his prowess went unremarked. He became bored with weaving figures of eight round the well-filled shelters whose inhabitants reacted indifferently to his display so he directed his bicycle wheels to the sunken gardens. Dismounting, he turned the bicycle upside down. "Watch this," he said. "I'll show you how the chain works." Winifred and I suspended our skipping to watch. Grabbing one of the pedals, he turned it furiously to demonstrate the chain's action. Then, to enliven proceedings by abruptly stopping the revolving wheel, he thrust his gloved forefinger into a link of the chain. The glove prevented his finger end from total amputation. We looked on in horror. His shout of pain caused mother such consternation she dropped her crochet work and ran to investigate.

Fearful of what she might find if the glove was removed, she bound up the blood-stained finger end tightly and Aunty Nellie, with great presence of mind, removed her scarf and turned it into a sling. One of the stalwarts from the promenade shelter hearing the commotion, hastened to help and offered to find a taxi for mother and Gordon to go to the Victoria Hospital in Blackpool. Winifred and I dissolved into tears and were absolutely useless until Aunty Nellie rounded on us to gather up the bits and pieces. She righted the bicycle and we helped her trundle it back to the hire shop.

As we made our way by tram to the hospital, Aunty Nellie speculated on the extent of Gordon's injury and outcome. She was optimistic the finger end would be saved rather than severed. In the event, she was right. The doctors saved the finger end at the expense of normality. It bore a mushroom-like appearance and many months passed before any sensation returned to the fingertip.

There was no sign of my mother or Gordon on our arrival in casualty. Aunty Nellie sought out a blue-uniformed

134

figure and made discreet enquiries. Gordon, it transpired, was still in the treatment room. But where was mother? Briskly propelling us to a cubicle, the sister swept aside the curtain to reveal mother horizontal on a hospital trolley with closed eyes and pale as a ghost. The sight of Gordon's dangling finger-end as the doctor cut away the blood clotted glove had proved too much for her. The nurses placed her on a trolley, covered her with a blanket, wheeled her into a cubicle and left her to recover.

"She's just resting," the nurse said breezily. Seeing her waxen and still, shocked us. In her bemused state, Aunty Nellie rummaged in her handbag, located a very small bottle of brandy, uncorked it and downed the contents in one gulp. This cleared her head sufficiently to make her realise my mother's needs were more urgent than her own. So, to make amends, she dug into the bag again and produced a bottle of potent ammonia smelling salts. Removing the stopper she held them under mother's nose. The effect was electric. Mother revived, coughing and spluttering. She turned puce and sat up. We laughed with relief to see her back in the land of the living. Shakily she climbed off the trolley and tottered to a chair. A nurse produced a cup of tea, hot and strong. The life force was sustained.

Presently Gordon emerged from the treatment room with a heavily bandaged hand, smiling wanly, his face as white as driven snow.

We took the tram back to our digs. It was well past dinner time and suddenly we felt ravenously hungry. Mother apologised to the landlady for our lateness. Mrs. Marsden quite understood. A kindly woman, she nevertheless had a tendency towards pessimism. The thought, she said, had crossed her mind that one of us might have fallen off the artificial cliffs at Norbreck or the North Prom, a not infrequent occurrence. Drowning she had dismissed, the weather being too cold for sea-bathing and the tide well out. Knocked down by a tram had been another possibility, but as the police had not contacted her, that too could be ruled out. Mrs. Marsden meant well, but her observations did nothing to make us feel less despondent.

She had kept our dinner warm in the oven and, though the food had dried out, we ate it. Aunty Nellie suggested returning home by the afternoon train. No-one objected so by three o'clock mother had paid the bill and our packed cases stood in the hallway. Mrs. Marsden accepted our decision to depart in mid-holiday with equanimity and charged accordingly, although mother did offer to pay for the whole week.

As the train took us home, mother and Aunty Nellie relaxed against the compartment's rough moquette upholstery and scrutinised Mrs. Marsden's charges. They discovered that, probably out of respect for our misfortune, she had waived the sixpence for use of cruet. They rejoiced over this unexpected generosity with such intense satisfaction that Gordon, Winifred and I, worn out by the trauma of the morning, and tired of staring at sepia prints of Weston-super-Mare and Bournemouth fell asleep with the sound of their repetitive exclamations of delight filling our ears.

The one rite of spring which struck mother as highly desirable but caused me considerable alarm was the singeing of my hair. The procedure simple and hazardous became, for me, a test of endurance. Mother, on the other hand, thoroughly enjoyed it.

Perching me on a chair in front of the fire, she grasped a hank of hair and twisted it tightly until I shrieked. By this time it resembled a length of rope from which sprouted frayed ends. Then, still holding on to it, mother deftly lighted a taper in the fire and applied the flame quite leisurely up and down the twist of hair until she was satisfied all the split ends had been burnt off. The process had to be

136

repeated until every hair on my head had been dealt with. The distinctly unpleasant smell of burnt ends lingered in the air for ages, though mother never remarked on it. In fact, she chose to ignore it, regarding every aspect of hair singeing as necessary to the spring programme and therefore there was nothing unpleasant about it not even the smell.

During one singeing session Aunty Nellie arrived unexpectedly. She appeared just as the lighted taper started its burning journey up a hank of twisted hair. Surprised and delighted to see her sister, mother began an animated conversation while continuing to hold the lighted taper to the screwed up hair. There was more than a flicker of panic as the taper flamed through the rope and mother found herself holding three inches of frizzling brown locks. Without hesitation she consigned it and the taper to the fire leaving both hands free to beat out the burning, fast shrivelling remnants of the twist. Only an emergency could have induced such extravagance when tapers cost tuppence a dozen. Without uttering a sound, Aunty Nellie dropped her handbag, flew into the kitchen and dashed back bearing a jug of cold water which, when it hit my head, hissed like rain dropping on dying embers.

The crisis lasted no more than a few minutes. They surveyed the damage. Only an inch of charred hair remained of the original rope and it stuck out like bristles on a brush. The stench of scorched hair filled the living room. Mother and Aunty Nellie assumed a casual approach. They hid the laughter which threatened to explode by gasping and exclaiming that, well, worse things happen at sea. When I viewed the disaster in the looking-glass I remained inconsolable.

In an effort to redress the damage, mother, after consultation with Aunty Nellie, took the scissors and cut the rest of my hair into an Eton crop. What worried me was the reaction of the girls at school. They would assume I had developed a violent infestation. In the end I wore a beret for two weeks to cover my disfigurement. Each evening mother massaged my scalp vigorously with almond oil until my head ached. Then I was bidden to tug the tufts of hair to encourage growth. Every alternate night the growing spikes had a shampoo. "When your hair grows again it might be curly," my mother said, with more optimism than conviction. She was wrong. It hung down straight and stark. Hair-wise, I always resembled Joan of Arc rather than Shirley Temple. At school I became something of a cult figure because I refused every inducement to remove the blue beret and disclose my dark secret. Word got around I had gone bald overnight due to a sudden shock. I never spilled the beans as to what really happened.

As April turned to May and the sun filtered through the layers of smoky, grimy haze, we expanded beneath its warming rays. Cotton dresses, dug out of the bedding box, saw the light of day once more, hems and seams required adjustment, cotton socks replaced long black woollen stockings and brown leather sandals replaced black barred patent shoes. Days lengthened. We played our street games, got ourselves filthy with dirt and tar, begged to stay up late. The lethargy of early spring disappeared, the fluctuations in the blood had miraculously cleared up and a tangible atmosphere of perkiness was felt in the air.

Spring eventually moved on to summer. Laughter was heard in the streets. Weary workers straightened their backs as they walked home on sun-filled evenings. Old women discarded their thick grey shawls in favour of thick grey cardigans. Young women walked abroad without hats but the men continued to wear their cloth caps and black boots despite the rising temperatures. Policemen sweltered in helmets and thick serge uniforms, patrolling the beat with perspiring necks and faces. However, the section of the community which truly welcomed hot weather were the very poor, like the Ainscough boys in Angle Street, whose perpetually torn clothing provided cooling ventilation to all parts visible and invisible.

CHAPTER 10

Summer

Summer began for us on Whit Sunday, the day the
Sunday School Anniversary Sermons were celebrated. It
caused a tremor of excitement and anticipation in the hearts
of the loyal members of the Congregational Church.

We bestirred ourselves early that morning. The thrill
of a different routine from the usual regulation Sunday
services was a stimulus to action. By ten o'clock a large
crowd foregathered outside the church. The deacons took
charge, marshalling some 150 people into an orderly
procession. It was no mean feat but they managed, after
skirmishes with the sometimes intractable Little Singers,
angelic in white at the head of the column, and the resentful
tail-enders at the rear. The older male members supervised
the body of the procession with a wedge of younger men
stationed like outriders at the back ready to intercept any
stragglers tempted to abscond. We paraded the area for
about an hour with everyone, without exception, dressed
formally in their Sunday best for the occasion.

The circular route round the district, was led off by
the Co-op brass band. Behind them a couple of stalwarts
balanced the church banner with its poles resting in leather
sockets slung round their necks on broad bands of
petersham. They, in turn, were supported by four rope-holding

assistants whose job was vital on a windy day. Without the anchorage of this quartet, the banner, and the stalwarts might well have been blown into a very untidy heap. The rest of us followed soberly, tranquilised by the vigilant presence of our Sunday School teachers and the dapper bowler-hatted deacons.

When the big drum boomed with the force of a 21-gun salute, we marched. At a pre-arranged signal, some hundred yards down the road, it boomed again and we halted to sing a hymn. While we were in mid-flow, half a dozen agile members darted about like dragonflies, vigorously rattling collecting boxes. Every house had a visit and the quick and the half-dead, the halt, lame or simply slothful slowly stirred themselves to donate a copper or two with the occasional blazer button or back collar stud as ballast.

Meanwhile the trumpets and cornets, anxious for the glory, blew mightily and drowned out the singing. Tensions ran high. As the hymn ended the choir master, determined not to be overruled by the band, mustered the forty strong choir behind the Little Singers and rendered an impromptu encore of the final verse. As the glorious sound of trained voices rose on the still air of a quiet Sunday morning, residents appeared at their doors in appreciation and the financial yield increased considerably. The band capitulated, toning down the brass section at the next halt. It was all heady stuff.

By the time the procession moved into the home straight, standards of behaviour had slipped somewhat. We chatted unashamedly, cautious reprimands went unheeded. Even the circumspect deacons exchanged latest cricket scores and the procession itself deteriorated into a straggling shapelessness once the band left us after the last hymn.

Back at the church refreshments and running repairs were required before we could face the shortened church service.

Then we filed into church. The deep sigh of relief as the congregation eased itself into the pews sounded like a

140

gentle incoming tide. For many the next 45 minutes provided an opportunity for a delicious doze. The well-filled pews on this special day meant a tired worshipper could snooze, upright and almost unnoticed, being well buttressed by his neighbours. At the announcement of a hymn the opening chords of the organ roused them sufficiently to rise with their supporters and sing-a-long with them, if they felt inclined. Afterwards they were free to slumber on until the next musical interlude.

Despite these irreverences Anniversary Day remained a happy and successful occasion for the faithful flock. As the most active Day of Rest in the church calendar it held tremendous appeal especially to the younger generation. All other Sundays paled beside it.

One year the regular rhythm of Sermons Day was unexpectedly disrupted. Normally a visiting minister officiated while Mr. Mayson, our own incumbent, went elsewhere. On this particular occasion the large congregation had assembled in church after the parade, patiently waiting for the minister to appear. Time passed. Nothing happened. A certain restiveness became apparent in some of the pews and considerably more than the usual number had nodded off from warmth or fatigue. The specially printed hymn sheets, spread out on pew ledges, were picked up and read, replaced, re-read, dropped, retrieved and finally laid to rest on any available space. Concentration waned as boredom set in.

From my elevated position on the platform with the Little Singers I had an unrestricted view of the rows of resigned faces waiting for something to happen. I watched as my mother methodically tugged each gloved finger end until she had both gloves off then she smoothed them and placed them neatly together on her lap. She managed to extend this little manoeuvre for all of three minutes until she caught my glance. I smiled and she frowned, gesturing towards her thigh. I got the message. My dress had ruckled above my knees. After my warm and rather sticky hands had ironed out the creases mother's brown straw hat inclined in approval.

141

The front pews were occupied by Sunday School scholars. There I spotted Ivy Ikin amiably poking a stubby exploratory finger up her nose. Ivy was a lethargic girl and no doubt her mind wandered off into a dream world whatever the occasion. Her outstanding feature was her moving jaw and I could see her cheek bulging with a sweet as she idly poked her nostril. Further along sat Phyllis Holden scratching her head ominously. She wasn't the only one. As for Jack Greenhalgh, squashed against the wall by the crush in the pew, his dexterous fingers had designed an aeroplane out of the hymn sheet and they were itching to launch it on a test flight.

A few rows behind them bright-eyed Mrs. Smethurst, in her best Sunday black, cheerfully wielded her hymn sheet as a fan, and further back still, old Mrs. Rigby removed her top denture and inspected it minutely before removing an offending foreign body with her hatpin. Once accomplished, her face relaxed into a smile as she replaced her teeth and discovered the bliss of a comfortable mouth.

By now, ten minutes had elapsed and a mass breakout seemed imminent. Just in the nick of time, Mr. Shelmerdine, our Sunday School Superintendent, scaled the pulpit to announce that the visiting minister had been suddenly taken ill. One of his deacons, Mr. Jones, had at very short notice agreed to stand in for him. Interest revived. Slumberers jolted back to consciousness.

Mr. Jones turned out to be small, thin and oddly featureless. His wispy grey hair clung thinly to his bald head. The crowded church appeared to overawe him and his nervousness manifested itself in agitated traits. His forefinger constantly plunged between his neck and high stiff collar, then he fiddled with his watch chain spread across his waistcoat. It jangled distractingly. The service got off to a twitchy start.

There followed the time honoured pattern of opening hymn, short prayer, Little Singers hymn, with a reading from Scripture coming next and, finally, the Long Prayer preceeding the sermon. At the start of this lengthy invocation Barbara Rushton and I tended to conduct a head count of the congregation. Our totals rarely tallied but it passed the time pleasantly enough. Unaccountably the closing words of Mr. Jones' prayer penetrated my mind and stopped me in mid count of the last few rows of bowed heads.

"Oh, Lord," he intoned, "do thou open the windows of heaven and pour upon us the buckets of Thy grace." He paused. The very extravagance of the metaphor proved its absurdity, though it stimulated the imagination. While I created the bucket scene in heaven, Mr. Jones suddenly seemed to recollect himself and attempted to justify this theological clanger. "For there are buckets in heaven," he concluded. Glancing at Barbara to see what she made of such a fascinating prospect, I found her still totting up heads, quite oblivious to Mr. Jones' startling request of the Almighty.

From that moment Mr. Jones lost his grip and when he got as far as the sermon there was further consternation. He took as his text: 'Come unto me all ye that labour and are heavy laden, and I will give you rest.' By some quirk of brain or eye it came out as: 'Look unto me...'. The error may well have passed unnoticed had he ignored the first word but, for reasons unknown, he clung to 'Look' with incredible tenacity. He spoke extempore and it proved to be his downfall. "Look," he announced, running his finger inside his collar. "That's what the text says, 'Look'. Well, anybody can look. I reckon there's not much effort involved in lookin'." Here he jingled his watch chain, while the devout in their pews rustled the fine India paper of their Bibles to prove to themselves Mr. Jones was misquoting. Yet they were unable to speak out and our man in the pulpit went on: "Lookin' is less trouble than walkin' or carryin'. And you don't need to go to school to learn how to look. Any fool who isn't blind can look." His hand wandered to his breast pocket, removed the white handkerchief and mopped his brow. Here was a desperate man. He had reached the end of his tether. "Now," he said grimly, "I'm lookin' at all of you and thinkin' of the text." Glancing down at the Bible his finger traced the next few words "...unto me all ye that labour," he read slowly and observed, "well I can see you're mainly labourin' men like myself." His gaze roamed the pews. Then with a sigh that came out like the hiss of boiler steam, he continued, "and are heavy laden. I don't doubt you ladies feel 'eavy laden with all you've to do, day in, day out, round the house." He was struggling, and though his remarks were intended to express his sympathy with their lot they had a disparaging ring because of his clumsy delivery.

An undercurrent of irritation vented itself in a rush of in-drawn breath from the congregation. He had touched a sensitive nerve. The men *were* hardworking and the women *did* know only too well the burden of housekeeping on a shoe-string budget. But on this sunny Sunday morning, dressed in new clothes, bought at a price they could ill-afford, this unnecessary reminder of their working-class status put a blight on their spirits. They desired glad tidings of good things, an inspiring uplifting message to give them heart to face the routine of another working week. Some intangible sense of their displeasure communicated itself to Mr. Jones for he hesitated, sank his finger inside his collar, rattled his watch chain and, perhaps suddenly mindful that it was, after all, the children's day, reverted to his original theme.

"Look," he repeated emphatically, "why even a child can look." His eyes fixed on Phyllis Holden now engrossed in unravelling the hem of her dress from a thread she had found dangling over her knee. Unconcernedly she steadily pulled at the stitching until Gwynneth Davies sitting next to her dug her in the ribs, pointing in agitation to the minister. Phyllis, looking up, blushed scarlet and the long white thread dribbled to the floor.

"You see," Mr. Jones went on with renewed vigour, "anyone can look, but it's no use lookin' to yourself. The text tells us to look unto Jesus. Look. Look. Look. If you do," he wound up, "he'll pluck you out of the miry clay and out of the fearful pit and set your feet on a rock. What more d'ye want? " He blotted his brow. We shuddered. The final part of the text, words which would have brought comfort and cheer to the majority of worshippers that morning, remained unmentioned.

The congregation, sunk in a collective depression never surpassed in the annals of Tonge Moor Congregational history, waited with stoical resignation for a merciful release. It came suddenly when Mr. Jones without any preamble said, "I'll leave it there for this mornin'," and announced the closing hymn. The sense of relief and release from this disagreeable discourse gave added resonance to the singing. After the Benediction the church emptied in double quick time. As we ate our dinner my mother announced she would not be attending any more services that day. But when she spotted my tears dropping into my rice pudding she relented. "Oh, well then,... perhaps I will go after all," and averted an emotional display.

The afternoon and evening services were conducted by Mr. Shelmerdine. Mr. Jones had disappeared, was never referred to and no one enquired about him. At the end of the day as we rose to sing 'The day Thou gavest Lord has ended, the darkness falls at Thy behest....' we knew that particular Anniversary Day would be memorable for all the wrong reasons.

On the last Friday in June, Bolton came to a standstill as the summer holiday week began. There was a lemming-like rush to the coast. For one whole week my father did not have to work. We packed our cases and went to the seaside. Our destination varied, but not much, either to Bispham, Cleveleys or Fleetwood. But never Blackpool.

'There's not a grain of sand to sit on' mother declared as though she'd experienced it.

Cleveleys usually won. Half our friends and neighbours went too so there was a change of scene, if not of company. Uncle Sam, Aunty Nellie and Winifred joined us, but not the Corkhills. Their summer recess was spent in Castletown, Isle of Man. Aunty Minnie resided there, and as Uncle Arnold, her nephew, deemed it prudent to keep in her good books, they stayed with her each summer for a week. In return she came to them for ten days at the end of the year.

Everyone went to Cleveleys for one purpose; to enjoy sea air, sunshine and themselves. Deckchairs, hired by the hour, provided comfortable seating for the beach. Sleeves were rolled up, frocks tucked into knickers, shoes and socks discarded. Sandcastles, turreted, moated or plain unadorned mounds, were wonders of invention and kept us occupied for hours. Tiring of sand we paddled in the shallow ripples as the tide came in. At dinner-time we had to return to the 'digs' for our midday meal.

On hot afternoons the beach beckoned again. More clothing could safely be removed. We donned our modest swimsuits and sunhats. Father and Uncle Sam knotted the corners of their handkerchiefs and covered thinning crowns. Whatever the weather, the ladies kept their hats on. The men took over the deckchairs and dozed. Mother and Aunty Nellie, greatly daring, lifted their skirts above their knees and paddled gingerly along the sea's edge, taking care to avoid being splashed. Gordon, Winifred and I, allowed only one donkey ride, cajoled until we had tuppence for another. No amount of wheedling though won us two ice-creams. By the end of a hot afternoon I became fractious. Sand stuck to my skin, settled in my hair and prickled between my toes. Winifred, who turned honey brown and never seemed troubled by sand kept smiling. My mother held her up as an example of how I should behave. Everyone left the beach burning from an overdose of sun. The evenings and sometimes the nights were devoted to applying liberal amounts of calamine lotion and witch hazel to fiery bodies. We bore the burning gladly so we could boast a rosy glow and peeling skin to our pale-faced, stay-at-home friends.

Those were the sunny days, rare enough to entice us all to grill ourselves more than was good. Often enough, though, the skies became overcast. As a special treat on a dull day we went to the Pierrot show, a jolly ragbag of entertainment ending with an invitation to the children in the audience to come up on stage and do a turn. Winifred and I, short on talent and self-confidence never took up the offer. One excruciating rendering of 'My Yiddisher Mama' from a large Jewish girl with crooked teeth and a voice like a 'foghorn', as Aunty Nellie expressed it, was so awful we severed our connection with the Pierrots for ever.

Wet days were a problem. The men, unwilling to take the tram into Blackpool, put on their macs and strode out along the promenade towards Fleetwood. The women had other ideas. When the men were specks in the distance we boarded the tram to Central Pier. The town seethed with holidaymakers and we fought our way through the shops. Winifred and I longed to sample the delights of the Pleasure Beach but our mothers, wary of such gaudy amusements invented excuses. "It's too wet today." "The Big Dipper would make you sick." "If you go on that awful Ghost Train you'll end up with nightmares." But more often the blunt truth was: "We can't afford it. Money doesn't grow on trees, you know."

Having effectively dashed our modest desires for thrills and excitement they promised us a 'lovely ride' to Lytham St. Anne's and led us back to the promenade and the luxurious Blackpool trams.

Lytham, the antithesis of Blackpool, demanded probity and rectitude, and like chameleons we adapted accordingly. An atmosphere of prosaic gentility pervaded the town. The shops, classy and uncluttered, lifted our mothers' spirits and sobered Winifred and me; we did not run or skip in Lytham but walked sedately, lowered our voices a couple

147

of decibels, subdued our laughter and upgraded our accents. The kind of leisured lifestyle it offered, appealed to the hearts of those who spent their days working in the grimy, sooty cotton towns. Our mothers were no exception. A few hours spent in Lytham sustained their dreams of the unattainable affluence, grandeur and elegance their own lives could never hope to achieve. Its influence lasted for perhaps twenty four hours. Then the dream crumbled and they reverted to their normal laughing carefree selves, until the next trip to this jewel of the Fylde coast.

Our childhood holidays seemed set forever. Then one summer we broke with tradition and spent Bolton Holiday Week in Scarborough. Gordon, at 12, developed a passion for camping. My father heard of a holiday camp on the cliffs of the east coast resort. He felt we should try it. My mother reluctant to change the habit of umpteen years prevaricated. The thought of 'roughing' it sent her into a decline. It was three to one for camping; the novelty of something different attracted us. We drew on every source of emotional appeal to persuade her and in the end we won. My father booked two large Bell tents. Three weeks before the holiday Gordon packed his kitbag in confident anticipation. Along with a pair of pyjamas he crammed in an assortment of scouting essentials, whistle, torch, compass, chalk and multi-purpose pen-knife. He aimed to 'Be Prepared'.

We went by charabanc. It broke down twice between Bolton and Scarborough and the sun was low in the sky when we finally reached the camp, tired, dusty and dishevelled. In the blaze of the late evening sun the camp looked impressive with neat rows of tents and a cluster of chalets. My mother softened slightly, and my father, hedging his bets, convinced us the mackerel sky promised the continuance of fair weather.

And for the first four days everything went well. Only a handful of white clouds floated lazily across the blue sky and an easy breeze made curly waves. Even so, mother resolutely refused to admit she enjoyed the camp. Our cases

148

remained packed, and each day she took from them only what was necessary. We did not grumble but my mother did. She cavilled about minor irritations, deriding the washing facilities and canteen meals. To all these murmurings, real and imagined, my father listened patiently and did his best to improve things. He rigged up a clothes line between the tents and knocked together a makeshift bedside table on which mother could rest her morning cup of tea delivered steaming hot from the canteen by Gordon, signalling his arrival with a blast on his whistle, at seven o'clock every morning. Yet almost from the moment we arrived it became apparent mother was poised for the return home. Every aspect of camping produced a negative response and when one morning she wakened to find an earwig on her pillow I thought we were going to have to send for the doctor to calm her down.

After a few days we made friends with the Hargreaves family, an ebullient foursome from Yorkshire. They occupied a chalet. On inspecting it mother immediately regretted her decision to spend the week under canvas. It unsettled her terribly.

A sharp off-sea breeze sprang up on the fifth day bringing with it large fleecy clouds tinged with grey. We played cricket on the beach to keep warm. Rain threatened as the day wore on and mother worried about the bits of washing she had hung out. Gordon had fashioned, with his penknife, some pegs from bits of driftwood; they were not very satisfactory. To appease her, my father volunteered to go back and rescue the socks and knickers, but the Hargreaves, optimistic and relaxed persuaded him otherwise. And when the sun appeared fitfully they somehow managed to convince mother that all would be well with her washing and the weather.

By the middle of the afternoon the stiff breeze had turned into a strong wind. Then almost without warning it gusted to gale force. The sky merged to a uniform grey. Huge white-crested waves crashed on the shore. There was a rapid exodus from the beach and even the Hargreaves family reacted with dismay at the sudden and dramatic change. My mother tight-lipped and silent clutched me and her handbag with one hand and used the other to hold her hat on. My father brought up the rear, carrying the cotton beach bag and the Box Brownie camera.

Dimly visible in the distance, the camp took on the appearance of a refuge as we toiled up the grassy bank. Our tents came into view and we paused to get our breath back. At that moment a squally gust snatched the smalls from the washing line and bore them like limp seabirds over the cliff-top and out towards the sea, never to be seen again. Gloom descended as my mother, chronically concerned lest money should fail, quickly calculated that at least seven shillings and sixpence had blown away. Anxiety inevitably sharpened my father's voice as he reminded her it was no use crying over spilt milk. Only Gordon remained cheerful.

During tea in the canteen the rain began. Great drops driven by the wind. We rushed back to our tents. My mother, anticipating calamity with each gusting blast, sat damp and disheartened on her camp bed while my father did his best to relieve the misery, tightening everything inside and outside the tent before dashing over with Gordon to batten down their own canvas.

The rain pelting on the tent sounded like steel-tipped darts and the gale roared with undiminished ferocity. About nine o'clock the centre pole creaked alarmingly as the guy ropes strained to hold it. With disaster in mind my mother had taken the precaution of packing the suitcases and extinguishing the hurricane lamp. Buttoned into our macs we sat disconsolate as refugees awaiting evacuation.

Soon the rain began to seep onto the groundsheet and one or two tent pegs gave up the unequal struggle with the gale and left their moorings. My father, on the alert, came to the rescue with Gordon in tow beaming his torch to demonstrate his efficiency. With a case in each hand and me clutching the back of his mac, my father and I floundered through the dense torrents of rain to the haven of the canteen. Depositing me there he returned to salvage as much as he could from our now uninhabitable tent. My mother and Gordon, shouldering his kitbag, swayed in unison through the gale after us.

Most of the tenters converged on the canteen and the staff rose magnificently to the emergency, serving food and drink and drying out sodden sleeping bags and clothes. The whole place smelled like an overloaded laundry. The Hargreaves squelched in, having viewed the migration to the canteen from the comparative safety of their chalet. They shook themselves like terriers after a swim. My mother had fallen into a dreary monologue about damp clothes and rheumatism so Mr. Hargreaves said in his down-to-earth way, "I know it's a right how-d'ye do but there's nought you can do about it, Mrs. Leather." And he laughed so heartily it brightened us all up. Then Mrs. Hargreaves offered mother the hospitality of their chalet for the night. She declined with thanks, believing there was safety in numbers. Anyway the atmosphere had grown quite festive. We were all drawn together in adversity.

The camp manager shot in through a rear door. He oozed bonhomie, and his touching little speech about the untameable forces of nature, the need to be patient and the desire of the staff to ensure the comfort of the campers drew murmurs of approval which broke into applause when he announced tea and biscuits would be served free of charge throughout the night. Finally he produced several packs of playing cards and board games and volunteered to organise a whist drive. The camp manager did a great P. R. job that dreadful evening.

For the first time my mother really relaxed. She actually laughed. My father heaved a sigh of relief. A broad smile spread over Mr. Hargreaves' tanned face and he rubbed his hands together gleefully. "The night is made," he said. And it was. Soon the call of 'no trumps' triumphed over the blast of the gale.

By morning the tide had turned. Veering east the wind blew itself out over the North Sea taking the rain with it. We stared out on a desolate scene. Debris littered the camp site, angled and fallen tents looked forlorn and uninviting as they sprawled on the soaking ground. Mother's euphoria of the night before faded and she wanted to return home immediately. With difficulty my father persuaded her to stay using the powerful argument of extra expense if we left a day early.

Overnight the camaraderie amongst the campers had forged a bond of co-operation. Along with the staff everyone lent a hand to restore order. By late morning the camp had taken shape again, bursts of sunshine and a healthy breeze aided the drying out. Optimism prevailed. My mother managed a weak smile.

That last evening, during high tea, an announcement from the camp manager informed us of a special event. At approximately eight-thirty the *R.M.S. Mauretania* was due to cross the bay on its final journey to the breaker's yard.

Well before the time appointed a long line of spectators gathered, three deep, along the cliff top. Children slotted themselves between the adults in the front row. The evening held that quality of stillness which often follows in the aftermath of a storm. The sea, smooth as glass, gleamed in the sun.

Suddenly the cry arose: "Here she comes!" Ripples of excitement spread through the crowd before a hush of wonder took over as we gazed at the awe-inspiring sight of a mighty ship sailing slowly and majestically into view. The prow barely created a swell as it nosed its path across the bay to its final port of call. The sun flashed on its stern; a small complement of sailors lined the decks. Binoculars passed from hand to hand and the silence was absolute. Grown men frowned with memories and emotion. There was not a dry eye on the cliff.

Early next morning the charabanc arrived. The bustle of departure kept us in buoyant mood. We had grown fond

152

of the Hargreaves and would miss them. As with most holiday friendships it withered through lack of communication. Though they promised to keep in touch we neither saw nor heard of them again. Only Gordon expressed regret at leaving. Heaving his kitbag into the cavernous underbelly of the bus, he pronounced the holiday the best ever for excitement. My mother, probably not trusting herself to reply, delved into her handbag and handed us a mint imperial each. Then she said, "Pull your socks up both of you and settle in your seats. We're going home." Her tone implied the prospect of home had never seemed so desirable.

CHAPTER 11

Autumn

The season of mists often reached Bolton in the form of fogs: dense, damp and sulphurous. At other times a sharp wind stirred through the streets whirling the flotsam of stray papers and dust in our faces. Chancing upon this wind on a corner left us gasping for breath and with eyes watering. There was little to enchant us when autumn folded us in fogs or whipped us with stinging winds.

A sudden drop in temperature filled my mother with a vitality born of seasonal changes and sent her to her knees in front of the deep drawer at the bottom of the walnut wardrobe. Surrounding herself with its treasure of winter wear was all part of the exercise. Out tumbled Chilprufe vests, liberty bodices, long black woollen stockings, grey flannel trousers and thick jerseys. Two piles formed. One for letting out and letting down, the other for the rummage sales. Once the clothes had been sorted my mother turned her attention to making garters, broad bands of elastic which acted like tourniquets on our limbs as they bit into the flesh. And finally the knitting needles, rescued from their summer recess at the back of the sideboard cupboard, held the welt of a new cardigan within an hour of seeing the light of an autumn day.

Yet we were the fortunate ones. In a house at the end of Angle Street, so strangely shaped it looked as though it had been cut off in its prime, lived the Ainscough family. The five Ainscough children wore the same clothes winter and summer. We knew Clifford best, he was a contemporary of Gordon's and sometimes they played together. The Ainscoughs felt the changing seasons acutely. They were caught in the inescapable trap of destitution. Mr. Ainscough, white-faced and sunken-cheeked wheezed his way up the street daily in abortive attempts to find work. His navy blue suit was shiny with constant wear. His flat cap had long since seen better days and his white silk muffler, grey with grime and age had to be tucked into the 'V' of his waistcoat to disguise the fact he had no shirt. He smoked butt ends of cigarettes picked up from the gutters and sought sanctuary in the Reading Room of the Central Library where the newspapers were ranged on racks round the walls and the warmth was the best comfort of the day. He perfected the art of appearing to peruse the newspapers thoroughly despite not being able to read. He returned to Angle Street at the end of the week with his step a little lighter having collected his dole money.

Mrs. Ainscough, colourless and careworn, struggled inadequately. She had permanently parted company with order and routine. My mother's attitude towards her was ambivalent. She was half sympathetic and half irritated, believing that if Mrs. Ainscough 'pulled herself together' she could do better. Nevertheless, Gordon was despatched with the usual batches of baking, insufficient for the Ainscough's needs, but accepted gratefully.

Clifford Ainscough was a friendly boy with a thatch of rough brown hair, which defied gravity and an expression bearing the imprint of poverty and deprivation. By nature he was cheerful and pacific but one day he became involved in a fight which indirectly affected us.

The reasons for the fight were unclear. What was certain was it turned out to be an unusually bitter and strenuous struggle. As the conflict took place on the cinder triangle, normally out of bounds by common consent, it created more than passing interest. Clifford Ainscough and Jack Greenhalgh were regarded as uneasy friends. They were like flint and steel, making the spark that kindles the fire. Most of the time they kept a brittle truce but this contest was fought energetically from the start. They began by taking side swipes at each other's shins, clawing at each other's faces and clothes until they drew blood.

"Ah'll brain you, Ainscough," Jack shouted. Clifford paled but stood his ground, grimly lashing out with both fists, his face screwed tight like a ball of waste paper, determined that, if any braining were done, he'd be the one to do it.

While Gordon and I stayed on the sidelines, Ellis Spragg took upon himself the role of referee, enjoying the fight from close quarters. He whistled and gestured at one and the other, awarding points and penalties as he thought fit. Mr. Bates's expertise with his walking stick and salvo of suitable invective would have settled the dispute in no time but he was nowhere to be seen. What would have happened if Mrs. Roscoe's mongrel terrier had not inadvertently escaped as she opened her front door, is anybody's guess. It was a sturdy little dog and rushed into the fray barking and jumping about like a crackerjack, snapping at the flailing legs and arms. Jack's nose spurted blood from a hefty punch from Clifford. In return Jack tore Clifford's jersey sleeve and the terrier helped matters along by snapping suddenly at the seat of Clifford's already threadbare trousers and dashing off home with the prize hanging from its jaws. The fight fizzled out. There was nothing for Clifford to do but take to his heels and run. Jack, frustrated at this unexpected end to the conflict, vented his feelings by throwing a few punches at Ellis Spragg before sloping off home, kicking the cinders as he went.

When the dust had settled Gordon went in search of Clifford. He found him with his bottom visible through the gaping hole in the remains of his pants, disconsolately poking the dirt between the cobblestones with a stick. With his jersey sporting only half a sleeve the outlook for Clifford seemed bleak.

"Mi mam says Ah'll 'ave fert' stay in bed a few days till she gets me summat to wear."

Gordon, surprised to see tears on Clifford's cheeks, for poverty had toughened the Ainscough boys, decided he could rectify matters. He raced home and bounded upstairs. I watched apprehensively as he came down with a bundle of clothes under his arm.

"What are you doing?"

"Giving these clothes to Clifford."

I was shocked. "You'll not get away with it," I warned him. My mother had gone to Mrs. Hamer's and we were alone in the house; Gordon blissfully assumed the depletion of his sparse wardrobe would pass unnoticed. My eyes strayed to the broad leather strap hanging behind the kitchen door. Though unused, it hung there as a constant reminder that punitive measures could not be ruled out if the situation demanded them. This would surely be it.

Two days later the inevitable happened. As Gordon and I left for school my mother came to the gate as usual, to wave us off. And Clifford chose that moment to jog into view, wearing his gift of grey flannel trousers, shirt and jersey. The fit was perfect. His dirty, ragged grey socks provided the only discordant note. We knew they started at his knees and ended at his ankles though hidden by the top of his black boots.

He stopped when he noticed us and gave his friendly grin. Gordon turned pale. My mother frowned, perplexed.

"Well, Clifford, you do...look...smart." She hesitated trying to make her mind reject what her eyes beheld. The moment of silent suspense seemed to last forever.

Clifford said: "Mi mam says ta very much fer t'clothes." Unconsciously he smoothed his hands round the shirt collar and down the front of his jersey, brimful with pride. "Ah've never 'ad a shirt afore." He glanced up at my mother. At least we presumed he was looking at her but his pronounced squint made it difficult to be certain.

"That's all right, Clifford," she said maintaining a daunting calm as the full impact of what had happened sank in. "I'm glad you like them." Her gaze settled on Gordon after Clifford, with his bare feet visible through his almost sole-less boots, sped on his way.

How Gordon felt I could not imagine but I quaked as I heard, in my mind, the thwack of the leather strap on his behind. I recognised the anger that simmered just beneath the outward veneer of my mother's calm. We were hopeless actors when it came to concealing any misdemeanour. Our faces reflected troubled consciences. We became desperate to please. We spoke quickly, hoping to get the worst over as soon as possible and accept the punishment which could mean early bed for a week, no sweets or comics, restricted playing-out times and at the extreme limit, going to bed supperless. This time the image of the strap being lifted down from its hook made my eyes water.

Then suddenly my mother relaxed and gave a sigh of resigned acceptance. We perked up. "It was generous of you to give Clifford your clothes," she said, examining Gordon as though he had just arrived on the scene, "but in future remember to ask me first." She paused long enough for that to sink in before exposing his unthinking carelessness. "I would have given him your second best shirt and trousers, not your best."

Jolted by this revelation, Gordon gave a little hiccup of dismay and attempted to make amends. "Anyway," he said, trying to enliven things with a bit of humour, "I expect Clifford'll remember not to wipe his nose on his sleeve any more."

The merest hint of a smile touched my mother's lips — no more than a twitch of her mouth really, and she did not allow it to linger. The mention of Clifford's nasty habit reminded her: "Have you got a clean hanky — both of you?" We whipped them out before running off at the double.

159

For quite some time after this my mother's appraisal of other children's clothing became embarrassingly suspicious, though there was no question of Gordon ever again repeating his generous gesture. An ingrained social snobbery existed on the subject of Sunday Best clothes; second best simply was not good enough. He had no Sunday Best for the rest of the winter.

Although my mother was generous to a fault in supplying all and sundry with food, gratuitous gifts of good clothes offended her sense of what was right and proper.

As for the mellow fruitfulness of autumn it was prominently and colourfully displayed at the Harvest Festival. Sundry items of fruit mingled with the produce of the allotment holders. Taylor's confectioners baked bread dough in the shape of an enormous sheaf of corn, and Mr. Adamson, renowned for the quality of his hens' eggs, supplied a carefully constructed pyramid of brown beauties which rose so high it swayed alarmingly when the congregation sang the harvest hymn, particularly at the rousing:

'Come ye thankful people come
Raise the song of Harvest Home.'

and the organist, beside himself with the joyousness of the occasion, got carried away, pulled out all the stops and thundered fortissimo the final bars.

Our humble gifts of fruit and vegetables went, along with the rest of the harvest yield, to local hospitals and institutions and the poor of the parish. One recipient was Blair's Convalescent Hospital and the Matron always responded with a letter of thanks to the church. There came a muted note of gratitude one bumper year, implying the surfeit of fruit and vegetables had worked havoc on the 'intestinal tracts' of the convalescent patients. So much so, the hospital had been hard pressed to find sufficient bedpans as the patients dropped like felled trees with diarrhoea and

160

became bedfast. This state of affairs had, however, been ameliorated by Mr. Adamson's eggs which had restored tranquility to damaged digestions.

The news of the success of the eggs was announced to the congregation from the pulpit, and Mr. Adamson, a most unpretentious man, deeply touched by the tribute, decided to donate two dozen eggs weekly to Blair's Hospital for a whole year. Mrs. Adamson startled my mother by saying it would mean their own supply of eggs would be halved by this generous gift to the hospital. Unsure whether to side with her friend Mrs. Adamson on this philanthropic issue my mother drew on her store of apt quotations: "Charity begins at home," she said and left it at that.

When Robert Louis Stevenson wrote that to travel hopefully is a better thing than to arrive, he could not have known how applicable it was to one of Bolton's pea-soupers. Before the end of November we often experienced at least one of these thick, suffocating fogs. Impenetrable banks of still, grey air built up over the streets, hugging the houses until visibility was nil. Sometimes these fogs came in clusters like late trams, and brought everything to a standstill. There were brave souls who set off trustingly for their destination despite the gloom, not knowing how or when they would arrive and with only a vague sense of where that destination lay. Walking in a pea-souper held a thrill of excitement for us as children. We remained blissfully unaware of its menacing properties as it enveloped us like a shroud until the adults punctured our excitement by spelling out the evils of fog in much the same way Mr. Mayson preached on 'The wages of sin is death'. Then we muffled our faces in an effort to keep it out of our lungs and when we blew our noses we found our handkerchiefs inky black.

One November Thursday, the first signs of fog began drifting above the houses early in the afternoon. Mr. Cook announced school would close at three. Five minutes after the bell rang Gordon and I were safely home. Then the fog really closed in, sealing the streets and hanging motionless about the houses. An unexpected knock at the front door made us hang back while my mother answered it. Uncle Sam stood there like a half-ghost in the greyness. Realising he was probably on the last tram to run to the Royal Oak that day, he hopped off on Tonge Moor Road and came to us, wheezing and gasping from the damp, soot-laden air, for quick refreshment. Determined to catch the tram on its return journey into town, he stayed only long enough to drink a pot of tea. As he sipped the scalding liquid he kept an eye on the clock and a hand on his inspector's hat hanging on the doorknob anxious to be on his way. For once he had little to say but the colour came back in his cheeks as the hot tea with, I imagine, a dash of brandy added, warmed him.

He swallowed the last mouthful and settled his hat well down on his broad head. "If I don't catch that tram," he said, snuggling down into his upturned overcoat collar, "I'll doubtless have to walk home."

We gathered at the door gazing into the murky gloom as he held his hand against the window-sill to guide him up the street and seconds later he became invisible. We strained to hear his boots on the pavement and caught the faint sound of regular steps sending back muffled echoes. It was impossible to guess the distance and speed of his progress. A smothered cough or was it a gasp took us by surprise. It sounded close and yet within moments there was no sound of Uncle Sam. He had vanished into the depths of the fog. The gas lamp outside our door cast a blurred circle on the pavement drawing up the swirls of grey air. "Come in now," my mother said, "it's not doing us any good staying here."

She closed the door. We were warm and safe. Our thoughts turned from Uncle Sam to my father. To leave work before five o'clock would be unthinkable, whatever the

162

weather, therefore he would be home late. In the event he was an hour later than usual. His tea had been kept warm in the oven and the kippers regularly moistened with knobs of butter. Even so they began to dry out between the plates. Finally my father put in an appearance, having missed the turning into Entwistle Street and taken a circuitous route up Ainsworth Lane following the railings round by St. Augustine's church before finding himself suddenly outside the Starkie Arms. He would have died rather than enter it. The 200 yards walk from there took a further ten minutes. "You look all in," my mother murmured sympathetically while mentally wondering if the kippers could bear another moistening. It was too bad that when she took them out of the oven they slid onto the floor, butter side down, but this was no time for niceties of hygiene. Scooping them back on the plate she added more nuggets of butter, and my father ate them thankfully.

Next day the fog cleared slowly, hanging about depressingly like a bad smell. In the afternoon Aunty Lizzie came and recounted her experiences of the previous evening when she and Uncle Arnold drove down to the Palais.

"You don't mean to say you went in all that fog?" My mother looked aghast.

"Well it was Thursday, Maggie, so don't look so surprised. A bit of fog doesn't stop Arnold. He goes even if there's a foot of snow. And if he goes I go too. If he stays at home on Thursdays, he's utterly impossible."

"Yes, but..., oh go on, tell me what happened."

And naturally Aunty Lizzie did. Arnold was insistent they should go, overriding her objections about losing their way, crashing the car, catching cold. She packed a torch and thick rug in the car and they left half an hour earlier than usual. St. Helen's Road was clear of transport and travellers to begin with, but soon the Lanchester joined a short cavalcade of cars heading for town. By tagging on to the end of this queue the Corkhills made it to the Palais and drew up outside the entrance soon after seven-thirty.

"What did I tell you, Lizzie?" Uncle Arnold said stepping confidently on to the Palais steps. "You're far too nervous about bad weather."

Aunty Lizzie, already worrying about the return journey kept her thoughts to herself. Once inside the dance hall the effects of the fog showed in the lack of patrons. Only the manager, three members of the band and barely a dozen dedicated dancers had turned out. They made the best of it for an hour when the manager called 'time'. Having been outside he declared he could not see a hand in front of him.

Back in the car Uncle Arnold accepted the manager had not been exaggerating. They set off, Uncle Arnold driving gingerly alongside the pavement. Three times they found themselves outside the Fire Station though, after some astute navigating on Aunty Lizzie's part they succeeded in reaching the bottom of Derby Street. Theirs was the only vehicle on the road, which was just as well. The fog wrapped them round like a blanket. By careful manoeuvering Uncle Arnold managed to steer the car on to the tram lines and persuaded Aunty Lizzie to walk in front of the bonnet and beam the torch on the metal tracks. That way, he argued, would be the quickest way home.

"That's what you said at nine o'clock," Aunty Lizzie retorted, "and it's now ten." Then she started to laugh her great infectious laugh. Uncle Arnold gritted his teeth over his smouldering cigarette, muttering, "This is no laughing matter, Lizzie. You're not doing the driving."

Legging it up Derby Street, Aunty Lizzie led the way with the torch while Uncle Arnold kept his eyes fixed firmly on the dull gleam of the tramlines, and never changed out of first gear. Progress was painfully slow towards Daubhill and home. With her feet aching and chilled to the bone, Aunty Lizzie valiantly plodded on, one minute peering into the gloom, the next checking the torch beam trailing along the metal lines. She walked mechanically. Soon the fog, the torch and tramlines merged into one. She stopped glancing

164

behind and just forged steadily ahead. As long as the torch trapped the tramlines in its light they must surely reach home eventually.

Aunty Lizzie must have fallen into a reverie because she could not say precisely how long it was before she became aware she had lost the Lanchester. Her shouts of 'Arnold' sounded feeble in the fog and floated away unheard. At that point it was touch and go, she asserted, whether to abandon Arnold to the night and leave him to find his own way home however long it took, or retrace her steps. She retraced her steps.

Where the tramlines bisected the railway lines at Daubhill Station she stopped. It suddenly occurred to her that Arnold had confused the two and driven on to the railway. Picking her way along the railway track she 'Halooed' several times but nothing happened. Summoning all her strength she bellowed 'Arnold' and was agreeably surprised to hear a weak reply. Following the sound she suddenly came upon him with his head poking out of the car window, stranded on the up-line.

Whether it was tiredness, relief, irritation or Uncle Arnold's pale strained face with a glowing cigarette drooping from his lips that set her rocking with laughter she could not say but it restored her sense of the ridiculous:

"The car now standing near platform one..." she hooted, and laughed till she was hoarse. Uncle Arnold coughing himself raspberry-red managed a feeble grin. They sobered up quickly enough as they thought of negotiating the return journey to the junction of tram and trainlines. With fresh determination and concentration they made it home in twenty minutes. The boys, hovering round the front gate, heard the unmistakable growl of the Lanchester and called out into the blackness, jumping up and down with excitement. Although Aunty Lizzie was indescribably relieved to see her home and the boys again she sent them indoors with tingling bottoms for acting so foolishly as to stand at the gate in such foul weather without their gaberdines on.

As for Uncle Sam, we heard next day that he reached the Starkie as the tram glided into view like the Marie Celeste of the transport world. It took him safely to Trinity Street terminus. From there his faltering steps went freelance, taking him on a mystery tour up Chorley Old Road, which, in the fulness of time and more by luck than design, ended at Lonsdale Road.

Socially our lives reached a plateau in autumn. Summer had departed, Christmas was still too far away to excite us. We moped about until the Church Bazaar, a three day event, beloved by the ladies of the congregation, endured by the men, adored by the children, and ultimately enjoyed by all, enlivened the dreary autumn days.

Preparations for this bonanza began as the previous bazaar ended, being an ongoing campaign which gave pleasure and purpose to respectable ladies devoted to flying the flag for the good of the church and future generations.

Apart from bed and breakfast at home, the bazaar occupied us from Thursday to Saturday. Officially opened by a local dignitary, buying and selling, and eating and drinking continued unabated until late on Saturday evening. An unending supply of home-made fancy goods, colourful bric-a-brac, or bree-a-braa as Mr. Sefton pronounced it, having served in France in 1916 he felt he had complete mastery of the French language. Cakes, biscuits, jams, pickles, rich home-made caramel toffee and real lemonade continued to fill the stalls until the final hour of the bazaar. When one lot sold out another appeared as from nowhere. We felt no guilt at all as we devoured the delicious goodies to our hearts' content.

All the ladies of the church pursued their allotted tasks with dedication, producing food and drink in the bowels of the church with no more than basic facilities. The gas water heaters, clamped to the wall above the sinks, steamed and spluttered out boiling water without ceasing to fill tea and coffee jugs the size of cauldrons. Gigantic pans rested on small primitive gas rings and bubbled with boiling potatoes ready to add to the stewed meat for potato pies baked in tin washing up bowls with a covering of rich short pastry that hung tantalisingly over the sides of the bowls, begging to be broken off and eaten before the pie knife could reach it. The wonder of it all was that no major disaster, no blaze, explosion, fire or flood ever overtook the event.

My mother, handing out piles of tea towels needed to dry the endless mountains of washed dishes, found the action-packed three days invigorating.

"Too many cooks spoil the broth," was Mrs. Clough's verdict as she moved with a worried expression to clear up yet another spillage. Her work-roughened palms grasped the handle of her mop so fiercely it seemed her fingers might instantly set it alight. Accustomed to having the whole building to herself in silence and solitude, the constant bustle of bodies, noise of excited children, spilt drinks, dropped food and the occasional over-indulged infant being sick tended to make her understandably tetchy. The general cleanliness and tidiness of the church and Sunday School was Mrs. Clough's responsibility and she took her duties seriously. The bazaar disrupted her routine so she was probably the only person who actively disliked the exhilaration of it. Her constant companions for the three days were mop and bucket, sweeping brush and floor cloth. Clearing the aftermath kept her, she declared, on her knees for a week, not praying but muttering malevolently at each new discovery of discarded cake crumbs, cardboard cups or leftover mushy peas. Her joints became as stiff as the Sunday School floorboards.

The best-selling book at the bazaar was the annual recipe and household tips magazine published specially for the occasion. Full of fascinating household hints and no nonsense recipes, my mother read it from cover to cover. One year an intriguing cake recipe took my mother's fancy and sent us all to our Bibles. It was Scripture Cake sent in by a Miss Palmer. A whole evening passed while we interpreted the ingredients. It took intense concentration and cerebral activity to identify the list of scriptural directions.

There were twelve ingredients:

1.	½lb Judges V, 25	butter
2.	½lb Jeremiah VI, 20	sugar
3.	1 tablespoon 1st Samuel XIV, 25	honey
4.	3 Jeremiah XVII, 11	eggs
5.	½lb 1st Samuel XXX, 12	raisins
6.	½lb Nahum III, 12	figs
7.	2ozs Numbers XVII, 8	blanched and chopped almonds
8.	1lb 1st Kings IV, 22	flour
9.	Season to taste 2nd Chronicles IX, 9	spice
10.	Pinch Leviticus II, 13	salt
11.	1 tablespoon Amos IV, 5	baking powder
12.	3 tablespoons Judges IV, 19	milk

Cream numbers 1, 2 and 3, add 4, one at a time, still beating, add 5, 6 and 7 and beat again. Next add 8, 9, 10 and 11, previously mixed, then add 12. Bake in a rather slow over not less than 1 ½ hours.

My mother never made this cake considering it an expensive indulgence.

The Saturday evening concert signalled the climax of the bazaar. Pretty mediocre stuff which, to our gratification, the audience applauded as though we were the Royal Shakespeare Company. And finally the Rev. Mayson drew the whole thing to a close, after commending the untiring efforts of the ladies, whose faces shone with heat and exhaustion, by embarking on a rather overblown prayer of

168

blessing on another happy and successful event. He voiced the same sentiments year in year out and they never failed to please. The church ladies' faces gleamed with reviving enthusiasm, as he breathed the final 'Amen'.

At the bottom of George Barton Street and directly opposite the Ainscough's house was a piece of spare land surrounded by iron railings. In the course of time these were removed to make way for the building of old people's bungalows. The workmen threw the rusty metal-tipped railings in untidy heaps on the building site and the boys used them as spears in their games of cowboys and Indians.

Clifford's younger brother, Rowland, entering into the spirit of these thrilling war games, as seen each week at the pictures, threw his spear as readily as the rest. In the middle of a particularly fierce battle one autumn day, the tip of a rusty railing pierced Rowland's left temple. He ran home with blood pouring from the wound. It was Saturday and dinner-time. Mrs. Ainscough, with so many mouths to feed and a kitchen full of steam, paid scant attention to the tiny slit above Rowland's eye. Her boys were regular victims of cut knees, black eyes, and bruised elbows so she wasted little sympathy on these minor accidents. Finding a roll of sticking plaster she cut off a piece just the size of the wound, smoothed it over the cut and gave Rowland his dinner. Afterwards, to cheer him up and no doubt to ensure some peace in the house she packed him off to the matinee at the Palace Picture House with his brothers.

During the serial instalment of the cowboy film Rowland was sick. The noise, mixture of vile smells and seething excitement engendered by the film, meant it passed unnoticed. Even if Rowland had called attention to his plight their guts were so gripped by the wild events on screen, the little drama of Rowland's sickness would not have drawn the blink of an eye or twitch of a nose.

By the time the Ainscough boys arrived home that afternoon Rowland was almost unconscious and, bewildered by it all, his brothers supported him under his arms to keep him upright. Mrs. Hamer was sent for. She organised an ambulance and went in it with Rowland to the Infirmary but within a few hours Rowland died. Blood poisoning, Mrs. Hamer told my mother.

Rowland, a lively boy, cheerful and tough for his age, had become a victim of time, circumstance and sheer ignorance.

A couple of days later I joined two or three other children in going to the Ainscough's house to view the body. Although my blood froze at the thought of seeing Rowland dead, I climbed the dark, uncarpeted stairs behind the others, trembling with fear. Mrs. Ainscough led the way. She opened the back bedroom door just sufficiently to allow us to see the coffin resting on trestles. Our eyes were riveted on the small marble-white face visible above the shroud. Rowland's skin appeared transparent and I imagined I could see the skull beneath it. The sight overawed me especially when I noticed the only visible reminder of the fatal wound — a barely perceptible scar on Rowland's left temple. His thick, black hair lay tidily across his forehead, his small hands folded on his chest. I could only think how pure and clean he looked in death. No one spoke.

We turned and stumbled downstairs. Mrs. Ainscough held the front door open for us. No thoughts of how she must be feeling entered my mind. I was completely absorbed by my own emotions. As we trooped out she said, "He looks lovely, doesn't he?" We nodded, too shaken by the experience to reply. I managed a shaky, "thank you." Outside the dull November air seemed suddenly as precious as life itself. I gulped it in to rid myself of the stale smell of decay that hung about the house.

On hearing of this excursion to a house of death my mother's reaction was predictable. She viewed it as an intrusion on private grief. Yet, while deploring it, listened with rapt attention as I described the scene in the Ainscough's back bedroom.

One of the Ainscough's neighbours toured the three streets collecting money for a wreath the day before Rowland's funeral. My mother gave grudgingly, declaring the money would be better spent on food for the living in the Ainscough household. But the ritual prevailed.

Neither Gordon nor I saw Rowland's funeral but remember the grey blustery weather of that November day. For days afterwards the neighbours came and discussed the tragedy with my mother but, in a surprisingly short time, newer topics of tragedies and triumphs displaced it in general conversation and normal routine took its usual course. Rowland's death was not an unusual event but the memory of him and the manner of his death has survived the passage of time.

As autumn drifted dully towards winter Tonge Moor Road library took the form of an Alladdin's Cave of escapism with its supply of books which we could borrow for a week with our brown cardboard tickets. Often it took us until closing time to make our choice from shelves of well-used books with tacky covers and turned-down page corners. The librarian, susceptible to any jarring sound within the precincts of the library, where silence reigned supreme, created a certain agitation amongst the borrowers when she firmly pinged a little brass bell to signal five minutes to closing time. After much shuffling of feet and a hurried replacement of unwanted books on the nearest shelf a small queue formed at the counter. The librarian, rubber stamp at the ready, branded the return-by-date on the inner leaf, removed the cardboard ticket and replenished the stamp on the ink pad. With our week's reading matter tucked firmly under our arms we left the warmth and light of the library for the gaslit glow of Tonge Moor Road.

One evening as I lingered idly among the bookshelves I noticed a young woman searching diligently along the ranks of books, pulling out some, pushing them back, scanning more useless volumes until she was biting her lips and frowning with frustration. Then the bell rang. Five minutes to eight. Wandering over to the counter with the latest *'Jo at the Chalet School'* adventure I kept an eye on the would-be borrower. Still she travelled the length and breadth of the shelves fruitlessly seeking an elusive book. After a final grovel along the bottom shelves she straightened up and cleared her throat deliberately to attract the librarian's attention. It brought no response. She tip-toed over to the counter and said apologetically, "Excuse me..." The librarian, dismayed to hear a raised voice in the sanctum of the library glanced up resentfully and mouthed, "What is it?"

Crestfallen the girl tried again. "Excuse me," she repeated quietly, "I'm looking for the Messiah." This time, the librarian, who had returned to her stamping ground, did not look up. "Aren't we all?" she said laconically and continued to plunge the rubber date stamp on the steadily moving stream of books. "But you won't find Him here," she added, drawing the next book towards her.

I was last in the queue. I looked at the Messiah-seeker and gave her a faint smile. She looked bemused, responded with a shrug of her shoulders and made a wry face before scuttling off through the revolving door.

The reading season extended through winter to early summer, when the urge to be outdoors took precedence over regular trips to renew or borrow books. Most of my reading was confined to the evenings. For reasons best known to herself, my mother took the huff if she discovered me with my head in a book during the day. She baulked at the idea of inactivity in the daytime. It was a throwback to her childhood. Daytime reading in the Allinson household was frowned upon as wasting time. I too developed guilt feelings, and even now experience a restless unease if I read anything other than the newspaper during the day. Old habits die hard.

CHAPTER 12

Winter

Winter gave us a new lease of life. Gone the dawdling that dogged the autumn days. Throbbing chilblains, chapped hands and cracked lips notwithstanding, we piled our gloves and scarves and hats on the pavement and made the most of our playing time. Outdoor games crackled with an urgency not just to create warm hands and feet and glowing cheeks but also to utilise every moment of fading light. And when our mothers called 'Come in now' in crisp, don't-bother-to-argue tones, the skipping and hopscotch came to an abrupt halt and we ran home, taking for granted the warmth and a good tea that was waiting for us.

In December only shopping stopped us in our tracks. Ingeniously well-timed for Christmas, shop window displays fanned the seasonal yearnings for impossibly expensive presents. The attraction of glitter and colour held us pressed to the plate glass windows long after the cold stiffened us. Our wild demands for Father Christmas to deliver an impressively large doll's house for me and magnificent fort for Gordon as mother propelled us homewards, passed with murmured comments of "We'll see..." though we realised it was a lost cause: our chimney simply lacked the width to accommodate such large toys. Cost, of course, was a minor detail in our scheme of things. Money did not enter into it. Gordon resigned himself to constructing a fort from his Meccano set and I was disappointed but content with three shoe boxes roughly resembling a doll's house with no front and instant access.

My belief in Father Christmas persisted until I was seven. Doubts had been growing but with no-one willing to enlighten me, I clung to the slowly disintegrating dream. Gordon's lips were sealed on the mystery. He gave nothing away verbally but adopted an attitude of superior knowledge heightening my suspicions that all was not as I believed regarding the existence of the genial red-cloaked, white-bearded figure who professed such a personal concern about our dearest desires for Christmas presents when we were taken to visit him in the Co-op.

It was my inability to tell the time which gave the game away. The big and little fingers, past and to the hour, the change from a.m. to p.m. muddled my mind and sorely tried my parents' patience. To help me overcome this stumbling block they bought me a clock, and hid it in the cupboard by the fireplace.

About a week before Christmas, when I was behaving impeccably and practising embroidery techniques in the form of chain, cross and the murderously difficult feather stitching with unnatural patience, the regular ticking of an unseen clock jolted my concentration. No one was around so I climbed on the sofa arm, opened the cupboard door and spied a little amethyst blue clock ticking away merrily on the top shelf. My father was to blame for this discovery. His uncontrollable desire for checking the ability of anything mechanical to work had compelled him to wind it up and set it going. The myth of Father Christmas dissolved there and then and Christmas lost some of its magic for ever. At the same time my elation at having broken through the innocent deception could not have been greater had I unlocked the secrets of the universe. Being 'in the know' gave me equal status with the adults.

174

Christmas meant much more than presents, the tree, tinsel and paper hats. The promise of special food was equally exhilarating. The luxury of chicken, plum pudding, and Christmas cake, my mother's delectable apple creams with pastry that dissolved on the first gentle contact with the tongue, the sugared almonds we cracked our teeth on and the familiar pattern of a family get-together. The grand climax of the festive season was the sight of Uncle Arnold in unfeigned jovial and anecdotal mood. Although its lifespan had the brevity of a shooting star, it stirred us all to generosity towards him, but that too faded like a cut flower. By December 27th his glittering career as a raconteur faded into oblivion and we forgot all about this Boswellian personality locked inside him until it surfaced the following Christmas. He used his gift to amuse us like a random reward for good behaviour.

Christmas was one time Aunty Lizzie kept a low profile and naturally Uncle Arnold took full advantage of the mere trickle of conversation that replaced the usual torrent. Aunty Minnie was the culprit. From Castletown in the Isle of Man she made an annual visit to St. Helen's Road for New Year. Thoughts of the impending arrival concentrated Aunty Lizzie's mind wonderfully and successfully killed her appetite for days. Minnie did not actually specify times of arrival or departure but Aunty Lizzie learnt to read the signs. The delivery of Minnie's tin trunk just after Christmas threw the Corkhill household into overdrive. Two days later a taxi deposited Aunty Minnie's small determined figure at their front door, often in highly contentious mood, if the sea crossing had been rough. Encumbered by heavy serge garments of a bygone era, and black baggage, her arrival created unease among the embattled Corkhills and their initial warm welcome faded into feeble smiles as she brushed aside their pleasantries and battered their ears with the trials of travelling.

Aunty Minnie, five feet three, wiry haired, sharp featured, compulsively cantankerous and conveniently hard of hearing was a widow of means, childless and ageing. In a fit of pique she had discarded Uncle Arnold's brother Horace and appointed Arnold her heir after his return from America on condition he solaced and succoured her in old age. This dubious honour was received with mixed feelings.

In preparation for the ten day endurance test Aunty Lizzie doubled her stock of pills and potions, adding a bottle of Wincarnis and tin of Slippery Elm Food to her survival kit. Normal routine was thrown into confusion to accommodate Minnie's preference for frequent bursts of energy punctuated by short periods of rest when she expected tea to be served in a fragile china cup — 'so she can crook her little finger as she sips it' Aunty Lizzie informed us — and, at the same time, deliver her opinion of the Corkhills' uncultured palates as they quaffed their liquid refreshment from healthy-sized earthenware beakers.

The punishing schedule Aunty Minnie set in motion was borne stoically by Aunty Lizzie for about a week when Uncle Arnold, noticing her fatigue, dropped hints to Minnie that she might care to have her trunk despatched for Castletown. Having been whizzed round town several times by the indomitable Minnie, Aunty Lizzie felt her whole future hung on the reply. "Speak up, Arnold, I can't hear you," Minnie cupped her ear in apparent deafness and Arnold had to repeat his suggestion two or three times before they got an answer. It came, in the end, with characteristic tartness. "Not before Lizzie's taken me to the Sales." "But we've already been, Minnie," Aunty Lizzie protested. "Ah, yes, but not to all of them."

So off they went on another tour. Bolton seemed a bustling, stimulating place to Minnie after the quiet backwater of Castletown. Once in the shops she spent ages fingering materials, flicking her finger nails against china and glass to ascertain their quality and testing every gadget she could lay her hands on. But she had no intention of buying, being obsessively cash conscious. These arid shopping sprees hardly dented her purse, yet every shop and store from

176

Whitaker's to Whitehead's, to Woolworth's and the Market Hall, came under scrutiny. Aunty Lizzie followed, faint yet pursuing.

Back at St. Helen's Road Minnie sat with her swollen feet resting on a pouffé while Aunty Lizzie, rendered almost unconscious after three hours' careering round town, made a cup of tea. Sometimes Minnie had dozed off by the time it came, her mouth had fallen open like an oven door, while her top denture, slipping its anchorage, had dropped gently into the gap. 'Not a pretty sight,' Aunty Lizzie remarked, wrinkling her nose in distaste. At other times Minnie clicked her teeth infuriatingly but her hearing problem made her deny the habit when Uncle Arnold pointed out they were rattling like a skeleton in a cupboard. Finding her impervious to criticism he resigned himself to putting up with her unlovely habits. "I'm sure there's goodness and kindness to spare somewhere inside Minnie," he said to Aunty Lizzie, "it's just so deep down it needs dynamite to blow it to the surface."

The burden of entertaining Minnie fell on the only shoulders available, Aunty Lizzie's. Seasonally inundated with funerals, Uncle Arnold stayed surprisingly late at work and the boys made themselves scarce as often as possible.

My mother and I came across Aunty Lizzie, with Minnie clinging to her arm, one January day as they headed into the wind down Deansgate like a couple of bent pins. They straightened up briefly to speak to us though it proved difficult with Aunty Lizzie constantly having to wipe her watering eyes and Minnie dabbing at a trembling drop of fluid on the end of her nose. My fascination with Aunty Minnie caused me to stare at this legendary Corkhill figure with unblinking rudeness. She looked as though she needed re-cycling what with her hair spiking below the brim of her black felt hat deep as an upturned bucket, the cape affair fixed over her long black coat and the reticule swaying in the wind on her arm. It seemed unlikely she had ever been young. Aunty Lizzie, far from her normal self spoke only of the weather, as Minnie impatiently tugged at her arm making clear her desire to move on.

As far as the Corkhills were concerned Aunty Minnie proved an acute social embarrassment. "I hope," Aunty Lizzie said after a particularly ghastly expedition into town, "that Horace thanks his lucky stars for his miraculous escape from Minnie's demanding attentions." Uncle Arnold, also stretched to the limit after more than a week of disrupted routine, surprisingly removed his cigarette from between clenched lips to voice his agreement.

The moment Aunty Lizzie waved her guest off on the Fleetwood train, timed to catch the morning departure of *Mona's Isle* for Douglas, she caught a Tonge Moor tram and presented herself at our front door with a face, my mother said, carved out of granite, until she had 'got it all off her chest'.

This was particularly true of Minnie's 1932 visit which had proved traumatic for everybody. High drama had taken place. It concerned young Arnold. Coming to terms with Aunty Minnie's forthright criticisms of their habits and foibles had upset young Arnold more than the rest of the family. The atmosphere bubbled like fermenting wine as even their manner of breathing came under censure.

"You Lizzie, need to slow down," Minnie said with crippling candour. "Your colour's too high. Learn to breathe deeply, count ten, hold, then let it go slowly out... out...out...until your lungs are flat. As for you, Arnold, I'm amazed you're still breathing at all, smoking like a mill chimney all day. What have you to say for yourself?"

The only sign of Uncle Arnold's agitation showed in two bright red spots of colour on his pale cheeks. "Nothing" he said blandly from behind his cigarette. "H'mph," Minnie snorted and turned to the boys. "Raymond needs his tonsils out and young Arnold has abnormal breathing because he's pigeon-chested and should have more exercise. All this going to the pictures is unhealthy." A dreadful silence reigned.

Out of the corner of her eye Aunty Lizzie, observing the boys in the kitchen loading their catapults with dried butter beans ready to aim at Minnie, hustled her unceremoniously into the camphor-laden front room, sat her down at the card table with a pack of playing cards and recommended a game of Patience. By the time she returned to the living room young Arnold had left the house without saying where he was going. A quiet, sensible boy, not in the habit of making life difficult for his mother, his leaving could only be the result of Aunty Minnie's devastating remarks.

For the first couple of hours no one worried too much about young Arnold's absence. Perhaps he had taken refuge with the Whithams but no, Raymond returned from there with negative results. Then he must have gone to the pictures. They sat out the next three hours in nervous agitation until they knew for certain all the cinemas were definitely shut. When he failed to come home by the last trolley bus of the evening rumbles of fear began to unsettle Aunty Lizzie, and she insisted Uncle Arnold should report his disappearance to the police. Young Arnold's name was added to the list of missing persons. In her distress Aunty Lizzie slopped rather too much brandy into her glass and offended Minnie by accusing her of having a hide like a rhinoceros and as much humility as a steam roller. Minnie took a nasty turn, crumbling on the couch in tears, her teeth chattering menacingly. "Lizzie, how could you speak to me like that?" she wailed, wiping her tears as they rolled down the ravines of her cheeks. Smitten by a guilty conscience Aunty Lizzie reached for the brandy bottle again and after a measured tot each, an uneasy harmony prevailed. Uncle Arnold kept calm, staying silently enclosed in a smog of cigarette smoke.

When a suitable opportunity for gentle persuasion presented itself, Aunty Lizzie got Minnie to her feet and up to bed with the promise that she would be wakened the moment any news of young Arnold came.

It was three in the morning when a policeman knocked at the door. The runaway had been detained at Crewe shortly after midnight trying to board the London train without a ticket. The bobby, obviously mystified, said, "Your son begged us to let him spend the night in the police

179

cells. That's a bit unusual I must say." And he removed his helmet raising his eyebrows questioningly. Slightly befuddled with brandy, Aunty Lizzie flapped her hands and said, with a slur in her voice, "I expect it's like home from home in your police station, sergeant." The constable pulled himself up to his full height at this sudden promotion. "Even so, it still sounds a bit of a rum business to me. Would you accompany me to the station?"

Uncle Arnold declined the offer. He and Aunty Lizzie drove down to collect the miscreant from police custody. Relieved to see him safe and well, Uncle Arnold was tempted to give him 'six of the best' but noticing his pallor and utter weariness, they brought him home to a warm welcome and a warm bed.

Next morning Aunty Minnie in pedantic mood, delivered a few acid comments on the trouble young Arnold had caused them all. This precipitated another crisis. Arnold vowed he would leave home again, and this time he said, with frightening determination, no one would find him. Aunty Minnie tut-tutted at what she supposed was an elaborate and empty threat. "Lizzie ruins those boys" she said, giving a wintry smile and clicking her teeth maddeningly. Instantly, Aunty Lizzie rounded on her and a rollicking verbal tussle ensued which ended in Minnie announcing she would depart the following day.

Weak with relief, Aunty Lizzie suddenly discovered her fountain of good humour had not entirely dried up. Burying the hatchet might be a good thing after all. She thumped the sofa cushions into slightly more comfortable undulations and presented Minnie with a cup of Earl Grey tea in a Crown Derby cup — 'greater love hath no man than this' Aunty Lizzie said with her loud laugh putting herself in the right. Then Minnie produced her 'thank you for having me' gift: four tablets of Knight's Castile soap at tuppence a tablet.

"It's the present of a lifetime," Aunty Lizzie ventured with mounting sarcasm, "such a sacrifice for you Minnie in these hard times."

Without batting an eyelid Minnie exclaimed, "Well I'm glad you're pleased with it, Lizzie. Soap is such a luxury I always think." Aunty Lizzie caught her breath. "Sure is, Minnie," she said lapsing unwittingly into her long-ago American accent, "but not in this house!"

Then lest she be thought ungrateful she threw her arms round Minnie in a spontaneous gesture of repentance and fondness which saved the visit from total disaster. Taken aback by this unexpected demonstration of affection, Minnie too relented, and with unprecedented generosity gave the boys a pound note each. Young Arnold cancelled his plans for absconding again, whilst Raymond said cheerfully he would buy an air rifle with his money which brought on a critical attack of heartburn as Aunty Lizzie considered the implications of such weaponry. Aunty Minnie's teeth clicked badly before an unexpected bubble of laughter set her rocking in her chair. It took what remained of Aunty Lizzie's breath away. 'If you can't beat 'em, join 'em,' she thought releasing a laugh of gale force strength. And for the last twenty four hours of Minnie's stay no one was in a lather about anything.

"She'll never change now," Aunty Lizzie wound up at the end of her recital, "because she's spared no effort to grow old disgracefully, and she'll probably leave all her money to the Manx Cats' Home." She paused for breath rather than thought. "In the end I did bury the hatchet but not very deep." And the laughter came out like a volley of rifle shot.

Soothed and rejuvenated by unburdening her troubles Aunty Lizzie prepared to go home and face the chores. As she rearranged her fox fur so that the little fox's head clasped its tail just south of her left shoulder, a sudden thought struck her. "Do you know, Maggie," she declared with laughter already gurgling up from the depths, "Moaning Minnie is so mean she'd split a currant in two." And having established this indisputable fact tripped off up the street, her shoulders heaving with silent mirth, clearly impressed with her summing up of Minnie's principal characteristic.

After vicariously enjoying the atmospheric pleasures and pains of Aunty Minnie's annual visitation, thanks to Aunty Lizzie's histrionic rendering of the distorted facts, the rest of January seemed unbearably tame by comparison. I craved the excitement of an Aunty Minnie who travelled from abroad to visit us and who would take us to the edge of doom. "Our nerves would never stand it," my mother reminded me.

During the winter my mother favoured productional pursuits suitable for passing long evenings. Like most adults afflicted by the need to set an example, she knitted, crocheted and embroidered, endeavouring to pass on her skills. I was willing but incompetent.

"You're all fingers and thumbs," she moaned as I dropped stitches, crocheted unevenly and tightened the embroidery thread to a puckering fist while impaling my finger end on the needle with depressing frequency. Drops of blood splattered all my stitching work. They gave it added lustre, I thought.

But, from my mother's deft fingers, knitted jumpers sprang in rich cable and lacy leaf design, mats dropped from her crochet hook in symmetrical circles and exquisite roses bloomed beneath her embroidery needle. My lack of patient concentration provoked her irritation. All I desired was instant results. Stitching errors I ignored as long as the end product reasonably resembled the pattern. Having a mother so meticulously proficient in all handicrafts proved a hindrance to both of us. Baffled by my insatiable urge for a rapid turnover of kettle holders, lace doilies and tray cloths, she found herself swamped by repair jobs.

"Just look at this," she exclaimed picking up a scarf with three channels of dropped stitches. I promised not to make the same mistakes again. Instead I made new ones.

Attempts to teach me crocheting foundered on the rock of abbreviations dotted throughout the pattern's instructions. Interpreting such things as: *d.c. 7 times, 2ce into 8th, 1ce into 9th 10th 11th, 2ce into 12th, 1ce into remainder,*

182

seemed to me to make a toil of what should have been a pleasure and only succeeded in strengthening my resolve to forsake these tiresome activities and indulge my preference for stimulating the imagination by reading.

Without wishing to emulate the denizens of nimble-fingered ladies wielding their needles with speed and skill, I nevertheless envied them. They produced fancy cardigans in a week, fine dressing table sets, as intricate as spiders' webs, in a day, cushion covers in an hour. I enquired about their knowledge of sums. Basic, they answered, no more than adding up and taking away. How then, I wanted to know did they work out such complicated patterns of crochet work. They laughed and tapped their heads. "It's all up there," they told me and what a funny girl I was asking such strange questions. They were transparently honest and thought me appallingly stupid, without actually saying so, and would have offered to teach me had my mother not got her word of warning in first and effectively put them off. I was never in danger of suffering from unwarranted self-confidence; however, I tried to redress the balance.

Knowing my poor performances with an embroidery needle grieved my mother I decided one January day to tackle a tray cloth without either her knowledge or assistance. I turned to Joan for help.

Between us we came up with a plan whereby I could spend one evening a week at her house and embroider to my heart's content and my heart was soon content when it came to any form of sewing. Mrs. Walkden entered into the spirit of the enterprise, taking me to town to choose a traycloth which I paid for with my Christmas money. I found just the right thing in Whitaker's. Anemones and daisies clustered in the corners and linking them together were garlands of greenery. The appeal lay in the simplicity of design and nothing more demanding than feather stitch.

Mrs. Walkden generously gave me free rein with her embroidery silks. The purples, pinks, blues, citrus yellows and gregarious greens I chose, mingled to produce some startling tonal effects.

183

Every Tuesday evening it was head down over the traycloth. The creative urge sustained the concentration. I took particular care not to plunge the needle through the linen like a dagger into my fingers, knowing how my previous efforts had all been freckled with drops of blood. The whole Walkden household became a hive of activity during those evening sessions. Joan knitted a jumper with flawless ease and Mr. and Mrs. Walkden grappled with a gigantic jigsaw of the Houses of Parliament.

Fifty minutes of silent uninterrupted work took us to 'break time' when Mrs. Walkden prepared a snack for Joan and me. Afterwards my powers of concentration waned but there was no slacking at the Walkden's and the flame of motivation drove me back to the daisies and anemones. Having put my hand to the needle I knew there was no turning back.

Towards the end of February only one flowered corner and the greenery remained to be filled in. Privately I told myself my embroidery reputation would be enhanced from poor to fair, at least, by this single-handed effort though there were moments when my spirits sank as I noticed Mrs. Walkden looking aghast as she observed the monumental stitches padding the anemone petals; and her eyebrows lifted in alarm as I drowned the daisy leaves in ravishing green. But wisely, she refrained from commenting and left me to make and correct my own mistakes.

The undiluted concentration and frequent frustrations when I strangled the flower stems in an abundance of stitches and overshot the edge of the anemone petals so that they began to look more like dahlias resulted in the inevitable wilting of my none too robust constitution. My mother, ever watchful of my health pulled down my lower eyelids, studied my fingernails, pinched my ear lobes and immediately doubled the dose of Scott's Emulsion, adding a daily dose of iron tonic. "You're looking peaky. I don't think you should go to Joan's so often. There's no reason why she can't come here for a change. Anyway Mr. Walkden must be tired of bringing you home every Tuesday evening. I'll come across for you instead." She gave me a searching look.

Realising this was a hard one to explain away I fobbed my mother off with excuses.

"Mr. Walkden doesn't mind turning out. He said so." I was protesting too much. "And I must go to Joan's for another week or two."

"Why must you?"

Perhaps it was innocent curiosity on my mother's part, though she had probably tumbled to the fact that something unusual was afoot at the Walkden's on Tuesday evenings. Without giving her the opportunity to put me on the spot with more probing questions I jumped in with: "We're doing a giant jigsaw. It'll take about two more weeks to finish it, so I can't stop going now." This half-truth went down well and my conscience rested easy since my mother condoned the occasional white lie as a necessary aid to happiness and harmony and that was good enough reason for me to follow her example.

She capitulated. "Oh, well then perhaps... just another time or two." However, it was a short-lived favour speedily loaded with restrictions. "You must be home by eight o'clock. Don't get over-excited otherwise you won't sleep." And the unkindest cut of all: "Remember, nothing more to eat than a biscuit at Joan's. You know if you eat too much when you're tired it makes you sick."

All those tempting snacks of Mrs. Walkden's floated though my mind and now I should have to refuse them. Ah well, only two more Tuesdays to go. The end was in sight like a light at the end of a tunnel. I re-doubled my embroidery efforts winding my way along the garlands of green until the last stitch was miraculously knotted off on the second Tuesday in March. The glitter of the needle's empty eye gave me the feeling that the needle and I had been released from a prison.

Most of the daisies floundered out of true and several anemone petals suffocated beneath a surfeit of slanting stitches. But it was finished. Over those winter weeks I had acquired a certain stitching skill, nothing startling, of course, but definitely an improvement, noticeable mainly in the greenery. With increasing accuracy I had crept along the stems and in fact, it seemed as though some hidden hand had been guiding me. Joan burst the bubble of my pride when she pointed to a cluster of daisies and said bluntly: "Those flowers are very unevenly spaced." My face fell. Mrs. Walkden, testing the heat of the flat iron with a wet finger, glared at Joan, saying, "Well, a man on a galloping horse would never notice. They look all right to me." And she took the traycloth and dropped it into a bowl of warm Lux soapflakes, squeezed it gently and dried it by wrapping it like a Swiss Roll in a towel. Her grey flat iron pressed the linen cloth and embroidery so nimbly that the crumpled and grubby work of art that sank into the soapsuds became transformed into a thing of recognisable handwork.

Shrouding the finished product in tissue paper Mrs. Walkden laid it on my outstretched hands and I carried it home glowing inside as I imagined my mother's words of praise when she viewed the inconceivable. And she was generous with her approval. Not one potent pause interrupted the exclamations of pleasure as she inspected the traycloth from all angles. She loved it. She loved it so much she placed it, still covered in tissue paper, in the sideboard drawer and removed it only for inspection by friends, neighbours and relatives. My embroidery light was destined to lie hidden beneath a bushel of linen where it mouldered for years and turned yellow with age. The full flood of my endeavours never graced a tray. Still, I felt vindicated. Although my mother, gripped by the urge to encourage me, suggested from time to time that I might attempt a more ambitious embroidery project, she met with such stubborn resistance she eventually saw the folly of her plans for me in the embroidery field and left me to my library books and less frustrating pastimes.

Now and again my father rescued me from handicraft traumas by suggesting I might like to go with him after tea 'on to the road' to have the wireless accumulators topped up or to buy paraffin for the kitchen heater. These short winter evening excursions I found exciting. The cold caused us to hurry, but once we reached Tonge Moor Road the gas lamps, strung out like stars in a gradually diminishing line, slowed us down and added a touch of magic to the dark as the pale yellow lights softened the shabbiness and tawdriness so apparent on the grey winter streets during the day.

While my father took his accumulators into Kay's ironmongers I sped with the penny he gave me to Higginson's sweet shop. No loitering at the window making weighty decisions on best buys because a permanent curtain of condensation hung over the shop window which the candles, set among the sweet jars failed to dispel. Inside, the gas mantles popped and spluttered. Mrs. Higginson, shaped like a life-sized Christmas pudding was normally a patient and benign woman, but had turned tetchy with cold.

"How much have you to spend?" she would ask curtly.

"A penny."

"Then if I were you I'd take a caramel bar. That costs a penny."

On impulse, I ignored her advice and chose Jap cakes and rose-scented cachous without thought of the blackening ruins my teeth might become, or the nausea that frequently followed a dose of such delicious sugary delights.

Should my father have to wait for the accumulators, we sometimes wandered up to the library and joined the silent readers among the bookshelves. It was always a wrench leaving the library. We could have stayed until closing time at eight o'clock but my father, wearied of waiting for me to choose a book, rushed me back to Kay's in the cold evening air. His anxiety to collect the batteries and get back to the warmth of home made him impatient. Then, with my hand firmly in his we left the gas-lit glow of the road and moved through the darker shadowy streets directing our steps to number 17.

In his late teens and early twenties my father attended the P.S.A., Pleasant Sunday Afternoons, at Mawdsley Street Chapel. In return he was presented with several prizes of books for his faithful and unbroken presence throughout the year. He was modestly proud of the novels of Marie Corelli and Joseph Hocking and Bunyan's 'Pilgrims Progress' propped between the bookends on the sideboard.

Intrigued by the P.S.A., we continued the tradition with P.W.E., Pleasant Winter Evenings, when Joan came across and we lifted out the Family Album of photographs and snapshots which charted the lives and times of family, friends and relations. Each year we added the previous summer's pictures on our P.W.E. and slotted them into vacant spaces.

Recalling our formative years, photographically, held us in thrall on winter evenings. Methodically we turned the pages and noted with astonishment details that had eluded us previously. And yet, I must have been eight-years old before I noticed a glaring gap in the sequence of family photographs. The extravagant array of portraits and snaps of babies did not include me.

Gordon was there, aged one, blond and blue-eyed in a tinted studio portrait, dressed in a cream knitted suit and arranged on a sheepskin rug, with his fingertips gently poised as if they were stroking air, gazing at the camera as though he were in the process of discovering his true vocation. Winifred was there, pretty golden curls framing her smiling baby face with the innocent touch of wonder in her eyes. On the next page, my cousins Ruth, Nora and Edith, a dimpled trio formally grouped on a stool looking as though the effort of sitting still had sapped their smiles. And, there too, a set arrangement of Raymond and Arnold in tandem, dressed in sailor suits and gazing into the far horizon over their shoulders. All the pages seemed loaded with photographs of other people's babies.

"Where am I?" I demanded.

"Well...let's see now..." A few pages turned slowly. "Ah, there you are. Look at you. Do you remember that?"

188

I peered at the black and white enlargement of Jack Davies and me. Looking unnaturally demure I had one hand tucked into Jack's elbow while in the other I gripped a posy of small flowers. The occasion my mother referred to was a mock wedding held at one of the church bazaars. Of course I remembered it. On the facing page was the photograph of Gordon, perfect as the bridegroom with Barbara Rushton, golden and cherubic, making an ideal bride. Beneath the orange blossom flowed a misty veil and the obligatory bunch of arum lilies rested in the crook of her arm. Jack Davies and I as best man and bridesmaid wore our disappointment rather well, in the circumstances.

"Yes, I do remember it, but where is there a photograph of me as a baby? I was at least three at the mock wedding." I pleaded with her for an explanation.

Equipped with a natural flair for prevaricating, my mother made excuses at first. No camera available, no money to spare for photographs, no time to spend hanging about interminably at a photographer's studio waiting for him to fix the lighting, the background and me. She rambled through the byways of pretexts until she came to the unpalatable truth. As a baby I was not fit to be seen. It distressed my mother to think about me as a baby.

"You were born," she admitted, "with a lump the size of a grape between your eyes. Most of the time I hid you away in the bottom of the pram."

That was not difficult in the days when prams were cavernous and always had the hood up whatever the weather. "Keep her bundled up," the midwife advised, and being an arch conformist my mother followed the instruction to the last blanket. Beneath layers of covers, I stayed invisible to all, whenever my mother took me out, except those few who had the temerity to peel away the corners of each blanket until they eventually exposed the ugly duckling slumbering in the depths of the bassinet. Not surprisingly their reaction of shock on seeing my disfigurement robbed them temporarily of speech. The kindest remarks were something on the lines

189

of: "Well, Mrs. Leather, she's coming on." And the covers fell back into place leaving my mother wondering what she had done to produce such a disaster.

To my mother's everlasting relief the lump subsided just before my first birthday and disappeared soon afterwards. By the time she had convinced herself it would not return, another year had passed. My introduction to the camera lens, on Jack Davies' arm, came two years later.

This depressing little tale of my babyhood was not one I relished. My mother would doubtless not have told me had I not asked, and having told me we consigned it to the recesses of our minds and left it there.

The black and white and sepia images in the album faded from memory once it dropped back in the drawer and only revived when winter evenings kept us by the fire and we wearied of purposeful pursuits, the compendium of board games and occasionally, reading.

The steam from the copper boiler curled about the kitchen walls of Lenora street on most winter Saturday afternoons. Winter Saturdays never caught us unawares, they were a ritual of long-standing. My mother and aunts continued a tradition begun before they left the family home of tackling the week's washing for their parents. Usually Aunty Nellie arrived first and made the preparations. There was a regular rhythm of filling the copper, lighting the gas burner beneath it and sorting woollies from cottons and whites from coloureds, grey or black. A bowl of starch mixed to opaque whiteness and a tub of water for the 'Dolly Blue' set the stage for the Big Wash.

My grandfather dragged out the mangle and immediately migrated to the living-room for the duration. Aunty Lizzie, dropped at the door by Uncle Arnold on his way to the power house of death, received instructions from grandma on what was, or was not, to be washed before she took her afternoon nap to the sound of the squeaking mangle and the hiss of boiler steam. If my mother and I arrived last she was set to turn the heavy wooden rollers of the mangle. Mother sweated. They all sweated in the rising steam which threatened the kitchen like fog. Aunty Nellie fluttered from one job to another, prodding the boiling towels, possing the woollen vests and combinations gently in the dolly tub, starching, folding and helping to turn the mangle. Aunty Lizzie took a more executive role saying her mobility was limited by her steamed-up spectacles and she supervised the operation with a cluster of orders, 'thin that sheet down Nellie, otherwise the rollers won't take it.' 'You can take over catching the starch, Maggie. I've done it long enough'. 'Those towels will be boiled to rags, if you don't get them out of the copper.' It suited her to play a leading role and, in fact, speeded up the work by being brisk and businesslike. Behind her managerial capacity lay the knowledge that at five o'clock sharp Uncle Arnold would arrive and expect her to be ready and waiting to dash home and get ready for the first house at the Grand.

As the kitchen gradually filled with steam, wraith-like figures appeared and receded as they moved from copper, to sink, to mangle with damply coiling tendrils of hair clinging to foreheads and cheeks conjuring up images of the Brönte sisters struggling through a depressing Yorkshire mist.

During the starching process Winifred and I would be cajoled into holding a tin basin beneath the lower roller to collect the liquid starch as it was squeezed out of collars and shirt fronts by the pressure of the rollers. When our basin was full we tipped it into the original bowl of starch and so diluted it ready for the handkerchiefs. Bored with this mindless bit of laundering we sometimes poured the diluted starch water straight down the sink. No one noticed in all the steam and muted gaslight. But grandfather suffered. His stiffened handkerchiefs chafed his nose and turned it the colour and texture of raw beef during the week. His daughters were left in no doubt of their shortcomings, and Winifred and I got it in the neck from our mothers for our carelessness.

By four o'clock the end was in sight. By five o'clock the washing hung on creel and clothes maiden, the range fire had been banked high with slack and tea.prepared while Aunty Lizzie mopped up the puddles on the flagstone floor.

"Arnold will he here any minute," she would say cleaning her clouded glasses. Her sisters heard between the words her growing agitation. Once, arriving earlier than expected, Uncle Arnold waited in the living-room for a few moments listening to the chatter and laughter rolling round the kitchen. When he could bear it no longer, he glided to the middle door and said: "When you've stopped cackling I'll take half a dozen." A deathly silence followed. Seconds later Aunty Lizzie came into the living room, red as a beetroot, lifted her coat off the hook and they departed.

As the front door was closing Aunty Nellie caused great consternation by venting her feelings in a surprisingly passionate outburst. "If you weren't so disagreeable and impatient Arnold, you'd make life a lot easier for Lizzie." The door slammed shut. "I might just as well have saved my breath," was Aunty Nellie's unruffled response and she went into the kitchen to brew up.

Winter was certainly the time for speaking one's mind even though the words fell on stony ground.

CHAPTER 13

The Undiscovered Ends

"Happy New Year everybody." Aunty Lizzie bursting with bonhomie rose to her feet and raised her glass of Sandeman Port. Her flushed face radiated irrepressible good humour.

"And peace in our time," Uncle Sam added more soberly as the rest of us struggled to our feet, clinked our glasses and took sips of our seasonal tipples. The date was January 1st, 1939.

No sooner had our bottoms touched down on the dining chairs than Aunty Lizzie sprang up again with another vibrant toast. "To absent friends." She downed the remainder of her port in one gulp. She looked quite comical. With her high colour and head flung back, her blood pressure seemed to have reached perilous levels.

We jumped up again, glasses raised, racking our brains over these absent friends. Uncles, Fred, Herbert, John and Aunty Agnes perhaps? Maybe even Aunty Emily? Aunty Nellie ventured, "Lizzie, you don't mean..." Her eyes widened with shock and wonder. She could not yet bring herself to utter the name Adolf Hitler. But we all realised it hovered on the brink of her lips.

"No Nellie," Aunty Lizzie retorted robustly, "not Adolf...Minnie." Suppressing the wicked laughter which threatened to overtake her made the flesh quiver beneath her modesty vest. "But you're right in a way. They're both little dictators." The pent-up laughter suddenly burst out and we found ourselves happily responding to the toast to poor old Aunty Minnie. I thought of her regretfully. January would seem a long dreary month without Aunty Lizzie's highly-coloured recital of Aunty Minnie's annual visit to St. Helen's Road.

For the first time in years the New Year's Day family gathering was at the Corkhill's. Just before Christmas a nasty fall had immobilised Aunty Minnie in Castletown. And, God willing, Aunty Lizzie hoped it would keep her bottled up in the Isle of Man for some considerable time. We heard how Uncle Arnold, on learning of the accident had ordered a telephone to be installed in Minnie's house. Suspicious of this new-fangled instrument Aunty Minnie put up stubborn resistance. She called it 'an expensive contraption'. "It's so much easier and quicker to send you a telegram, Arnold," she said cherishing the tried and trusted methods of communication. Uncle Arnold insisted, and won. He rang her several times during breaks from polishing his best beech coffins. After amazingly long and crackling delays the operator got through to Castletown. Aunty Minnie, completely overcome by the marvel of hearing the apparatus ring, snatched up the receiver and, before the operator could speak, gripped the mouthpiece and shouted into it, "Is anybody there?" Unless a voice answered immediately she hung up and the whole lengthy procedure had to be repeated. Uncle Arnold's patience wore thin and he began to wonder what had made him think the telephone was such a good idea in the first place. No doubt Minnie had been right. A telegram would have been less costly and infinitely speedier.

The meal that New Year's Day took almost three hours to serve, eat and clear away. The turkey, buttered and basted and covered with streaky bacon was roasted to perfection; the trifle; a rich medley of sponges, fruit, sherry, almonds and two inches of whipped cream topping them all proved irresistible and the meal ended with Aunty Lizzie's gastronomic speciality, mince pies covered with a dome of meringue. The coffee and port which followed concluded a memorable meal. Aunty Lizzie, in her elation had excelled herself. Over indulgence brings its own rewards. During the evening Aunty Lizzie frequently resorted to her stomach powders. Winifred was inconveniently sick and Uncle Sam had a dizzy do. Gordon developed a convincing headache which gave him blue bags under his eyes and my mother had to usher me out to the back garden and encourage me to breathe deeply until the troublesome wind stuck like a stone inside me rumbled freely into the night air.

In between these natural breaks the inevitable card games got under way though Aunty Lizzie's high spirits kept us all in a state of inattention. Nobody knew who had won or, more importantly, who had lost. We all applied for a prize and after a tubful of trinkets had been handed out, exchanged, argued over, and returned to the original recipient, we were ready to go home. We left late. As the tram lurched along Bradshawgate and downhill past Preston's jewellers, we let ourselves heel over with it as corners were taken at high speed. When we stepped off the tram on Tonge Moor Road we felt like bits of seaweed flung about on a high tide. Still, it had been an exceptionally successful New Year's Day, my mother said as she removed the hatpins from her plant pot of a hat, but she fervently hoped Aunty Lizzie would not put in an appearance the next day. "I've had enough hilarity to last me the rest of this week," she said feelingly. "Minnie's absence has gone to Lizzie's head. She's bound to pay a price for all this excitement." Too tired to bend our minds round that ominous prediction we went to bed leaving my father to rake out the ashes and lay the fire for the morning while my mother, realising there would be no response to her remarks, set the table for breakfast and climbed the stairs after us.

195

No man is an island and even in our young and egotistical world the rumours of war, which spread daily, became a topic of formless discussion amongst us. We grappled inconclusively with the possible consequences of global hostilities. The playing field shelter at Tonge Park became the forum for the opinions of the brash and ill-informed youths eager to impress anyone willing to listen. The Germans would bomb us out of town, off the face of the earth, blow us to smithereens. Then where would we be? Gordon wanted to know. Up a gum tree, said Norman Rushton who, with his matter-of-fact approach, always brought us down to earth. No one offered anything more positive than that and we went about our daily lives with the threat of war far from uppermost in our minds.

My greatest pleasure was tennis. I lived and breathed it. Feeling she was being used as a landlady, my mother, asked if I should like to take the camp bed to the tennis hut and sleep there. Suddenly conscience-stricken I offered to do the washing up once a week. Three times a week or else... was my mother's reaction. Or else? The ultimatum was once a week plus the ironing. Piece work suited me better and I agreed to it. But, as my mind and heart were still set on tennis, it wore my mother down because I did my chores so carelessly she was glad to relieve me of them.

Gordon took to the road. He cycled the length and breadth of Belmont, Bradshaw and Turton until he got housemaid's knee then played the piano until it healed. Pedalling and the piano both gave him pleasure. For his fifteenth birthday my father bought him a cricket bat. This became his problem. He clipped Fred Smethurst over the left ear with it which brought Mr. Smethurst, in a smouldering temper to see my father with the alarming news

196

that Fred might be deaf for life. And what was my father going to do about it? What could he do other than fulminate and threaten dire consequences to Gordon should Fred be disabled for life. Gordon swore it was an accident and though my father believed him it so occupied his mind he moved about like a man condemned to capital punishment. My mother went into a decline. Two days after the event my father walked up to Smethurst's to see how Fred was faring. When the injured victim answered the door, grinning from ear to ear, and replied chirpily to a quiet enquiry after his hearing, the relief to my father, who had a fastidious conscience about matters relating to trouble and upset, was such that he pressed a florin into Fred's hand. And Fred, not wishing to lose the advantage, said he still suffered from headaches every day. This brought another shilling. But before Fred could think up other lingering symptoms my father put his purse back in his pocket. "Glad to find there's no damage done, Fred." And when he arrived home his first words to Gordon were: "I'm telling you now, watch your step in future with Fred." The new cricket bat was seldom used after that. Instead Gordon turned his hand to woodwork with the application of a craftsman.

Despite the troubled political present some things appeared set fair for ever. School for instance. School routine continued unabated. The hallowed Morning Assembly remained constant, with late arrivals allowed in at the end like a flock of erring sheep and herded into a conspicuous area as an outstanding example of slothfulness. Homework pursued us inexorably and the thought of detention kept our noses to the grindstone. After my early confrontation with Miss Hoyle my behaviour, within a radius of half a mile of school, never breached the rules laid down by her that morning when Ethel and I faced her in her study.

Throughout the school year our nether regions continued to benefit from the all-round protection from navy blue, fleecy-lined, double-gusseted knickers. They remained de rigeur for gym as we leap-frogged over the horse, vaulted

197

over the box and balanced precariously on the horizontal bars. During one session of vaulting the long, leather-topped box, Brenda Knowles, behind me in the queue, whispered in my ear as I stood poised ready for the run-up to the springboard, "Mind you don't split your infinitive," which made me hesitate. I set off on the wrong foot and pulled up just short of the springboard like a horse refusing a fence.

"Get to the back of the line," the teacher barked. "If you weren't so busy talking you would have made it. Next." Brenda fared rather better, but not much. Jumping heavily on the tip of the springboard denied her the lift-off she needed and I looked over my shoulder to see her straddled inelegantly across the middle of the box. Judging by her expression, splitting one's infinitive was an extremely painful experience. Yet, the all-enveloping bloomers shielding her thighs saved her from some very nasty abrasions.

Those members of staff we disliked rarely did us a favour by seeking new posts elsewhere. They were as loyal a bunch of teachers as ever gathered in their graduation gowns in front of a blackboard. Some of them, of course, disliked us with equal intensity. Our boredom and inattention, which we took no pains to hide, visibly affected them, making them sarcastic and intolerant, and their response to pupils who were boldly provocative bordered on the murderous.

Mr. Gerard, our French master, had more than his share of the Gallic temperament. His short, dapper figure turned rigid with irritation if any of us showed signs of drifting concentration. His small grey moustache twitched and bristled, signalling imminent explosion, usually in French. I got on well with him and enjoyed his lessons. Because his fiery temper normally vented itself on others, I became complacent. During one of his lessons, I was sitting at the end of the back row, and Mr. Gerard called out my name and asked me to translate into French the sentences he had written on the blackboard. What he did not know, and I only vaguely at the time, was a mouse had crept into my attaché case and begun to nibble at my sandwiches.

198

Distracted by the sound of rustling greaseproof paper as the mouse chewed its way to my mother's home made bread, I failed to stand up. Mr. Gerard remonstrated. I paid no attention. The classroom was silent. Suddenly he snapped, "Stand up girl." Slowly I got to my feet, looking pained and miserable. "Translate" he thundered. I made a hash of it, which produced a flow of French phrases from Mr. Gerard quite alien to my ears. Then reverting to English he dished out the punishment. "Conjugate five reflexive verbs in the present, future and perfect tenses. Tonight!"

That afternoon, going home dinnerless and disagreeable, I flounced into the kitchen, rattling the latch with unnecessary vigour. My mother, with her back to me, was transferring a batch of hot scones from baking tray to wire rack. "I can tell it has been one of those days," she said not turning round as she scooped the last scones onto the rack.

"Sometimes, mother, you seem to have eyes in the back of your head," I said peevishly.

"I have," she replied, "and excellent hearing too. Take your things off. You'll feel better after tea."

The delicious aroma from the newly-baked scones, the cosy warmth of the kitchen, and knowing my mother was just THERE understanding my misery when she heard about the day's disaster, helped to put me in a much happier frame of mind. No one could ever settle my world into rightness in quite the same way as my mother.

Next morning I handed in my work. Mr. Gerard, gently stroking his moustache, asked me for an explanation of my poor performance of the previous day. I told him about the mouse. He shook his head and smiled. "Mon Dieu," he said, "why on earth didn't you speak up at the time? You could have saved yourself all that extra homework." "Mon Dieu," I thought," I cannot answer that even in English!"

At the beginning of the school year, September 1938, a young, handsome German master came to teach us the language. He enjoyed great popularity amongst us. His good

199

looks, attractive, strongly-accented English, his habit of clicking his heels when we shook his hand as we filed out of the classroom and his pleasing personality ensured our undivided attention in his lessons. Eager to please such a courteous Adonis, we worked like Trojans for the delight of receiving an aristocratic nod of approval. The slightest inclination of his head made us feel we had received the equivalent of a Distinction in School Certificate. Herr Dieter accepted our adulation with Teutonic reserve. There was far more to him than met our unsuspicious eyes.

When he bade us "Guten Tag" at the close of the summer term in 1939 we failed to realise he was saying good-bye for ever. His disappearance heightened our fevered fantasies. Time was travelling by secret currents, and with a single purpose, to disrupt our lives though our perceptions of the reality of war were tentative and insubstantial. For most of us the concept of war combined excitement with fear of the unknown. We knew we were helpless to change the course of destiny. Yet with the resilience and optimism of youth we shrugged off the darker aspects of a world conflict.

The permanence of Monday as washday was still absolute in 1939. The only change in procedure came in the form of a Hotpoint washing machine. Designed like a miniature oil rig on wheels, it had rubber rollers which burst apart when anything thicker than two folded damask serviettes was fed into them. Still, it streamlined the drudgery even if it failed to persuade my mother that other days of the week could be designated wash days. Coalmen, dustmen and the rag and bone man steered clear of the back streets on Mondays, aware of the rollicking the irate housewives had in store for them if they dared show their faces among the lines of pristine washing. Venturing over the minefields of backstreet washing lines demanded nerves of steel and few there were who took up the challenge. Those who did seldom repeated such a breach of the unwritten washing day rules.

These sturdy certainties of life stayed constant throughout the '30s. If we were impatient for change we were careful not to show it for we felt helpless to alter anything from the time-honoured tradition of generations. Only minor deviations from routine occurred. Holidays, for example. Our tri-annual trips to the Fylde Coast gradually faded as holiday horizons extended to the North Wales coast, Kimnel Bay and Llandudno, and in the summer of 1939 we sailed abroad to the Isle of Man. The small unspoilt town of Port Erin, straggling a curved bay, captured our imagination the moment we saw it. Uncrowded, uncluttered and with white cottages set about with bright fuschia hedges, which perpetuated the timeless atmosphere of relaxed tranquility. Unhurried and peaceful — we loved it. As far as I remember, Aunty Minnie never featured in our conversation and a visit to her was not even contemplated. But then we were not alone on this holiday. The Ainscows shared it with us. Ethel and I, drawn together in adversity during our first year at the 'Muni' remained friends. Bob Ainscow and Gordon, also contemporaries, were both brief in conversation which made them ideal companions. Our parents got on well together.

Towards the end of the week a touch of excitement enlivened the holiday. We were all on the beach when Mr. Ainscow, screwing his eyes against the morning sun, said, "There's a cloud of black smoke billowing over the promenade." Sensing drama we set off to find the source of the smoke, now rising like a pillar somewhere behind the promenade. We arrived at the fire to find a crowd of curious spectators responding badly to the perspiring bobby's single-handed attempt to keep them in order. "Keep back there," he said, spreading wide his arms in a gesture of determined supervision.

No dazzling display of flames shot in the air, no roof fell in and only a couple of forlorn figures stood by the smouldering chip shop lean-to. It was like arriving for a grand performance only to discover the best of it was over. Still, with nothing better to do we hung about with the rest of the gawping bystanders.

Mr. Ainscow was adept at talking to anyone and everyone. He approached a bullet-headed man on the edge of the crowd. Tapping him lightly on the shoulder Mr. Ainscow asked, "Can you tell us what's happening?"

"Nothing," he said without looking round.

"Is anything being done?" Mr. Ainscow, a Bolton councillor, persisted as though he were at a council meeting demanding evidence of serious mismanagement of public funds.

The bullet-head swivelled sufficiently to fix Mr. Ainscow with a haughty stare. "If that is a criticism," he said loftily, "let me inform you, we have taken all necessary steps consistent with prudence and urgency to extinguish this fire. We now await the arrival of the fire engine."

After about five minutes the clop of horses' hooves reached our ears and the glory of Port Erin put in an appearance, a horse-drawn dustcart doubling up as fire engine. The volunteer force of six strong men and true wrestled manfully with hosepipe and buckets. Out of practice, out of breath and out of step with each other in co-ordination of movement, the smouldering out-house tested their capacities to the limit. After a disorganised struggle the situation came under control.

Mr. Ainscow was moved to remark loudly, "It's a thundering good job it isn't a conflagration."

"Well, sir," the constable said setting his helmet to rights as the crowd melted away, "we could always call on other fire engines. In the last ten years we've fought three fires, pumped out several sinking boats and rescued twenty two cats stranded up trees. We don't expect anything more drastic in the future. Everybody is very careful here."

202

Regrettably Mr. Ainscow had no ready answer to that but I saw him catch my father's eye and wink. We prepared to drift back to the beach. Ethel pulled up her ankle socks, smoothed them against her legs and then concertinaed them neatly round her ankles again.

"Race you to the beach," She said straightening up.

By the time we reached the shore Ethel was not only out of breath but hiccuping violently. We waited for our mothers. "Ethel's got hiccups," I called to Mrs. Ainscow as she and my mother leisurely descended the stone steps from the promenade. Immersed in conversation she did not hear.

"Mrs. Ainscow..." I tried again, ten decibels louder and more insistently.

She waved. "I can hear her," she said calmly, not hurrying but still listening to what my mother was saying. Coming up to us at last she dropped her handbag on the sand, pinched Ethel's nostrils between her right thumb and forefinger while with her free hand she gave her back a hearty thump. It brought tears to Ethel's eyes.

Then Mrs. Ainscow picked up her handbag and resumed, "Did you say Regulo 4 for cowheel pie?" and walked off with my mother deep in conversation on the niceties of perfect pie pastry, while Ethel, limp from having had the breath knocked out of her gave a great gasp and stopped hiccuping. "I must say you're not soft, Ethel," I said admiringly. Ethel wiped her eyes with a final hiccup of satisfaction. My remark made her feel good.

As we sailed out of Douglas at the end of the week into choppy seas, no promises were made about a future return to Port Erin. No promises were made about anything in the summer of 1939. Ahead lay uncertainty. We could only wonder and wait. Old men spelled out the perils of war as they sat contentedly puffing at their pipes on bowling green benches. They had seen it all before but this time, they said nodding gravely, it would be a war to end all wars. Nearing the end of their lives they could sit safely on the sidelines and make sententious pronouncements. A feeling of unease pervaded even the most innocuous remarks.

At 11 o'clock on the morning of Sunday September 3rd, 1939 we were all at home. Gordon was in the backyard with his cycle upside down fixing a new inner tube, I had gone into the garden simply to pass the time, and my mother and father who had stayed indoors called us in when the expected announcement came over the wireless that the country had declared war on Germany. There was no going back.

"What will it mean?" I asked. I imagined an immediate air-raid, a stick of bombs falling, with number nine Abingdon Road receiving a direct hit. Oh, the drama of it. Fleetingly I wondered if the safest place in the house during an air raid was under the stairs.

"It means," my mother said slowly, "that nothing will ever be the same again." For my mother to admit that change, profound and radical, was a probability, rather over-awed me. Yet I remember the subdued elation at the prospect of a new and altogether different lifestyle. It was as though a key had suddenly been turned to lock away the past securely. From this day forward the direction of everyone's life moved out to the undiscovered ends.

But for now we felt all at sea. My mother made the first move, "It's no use sitting here doing nothing," she said. "The dinner's nearly ready. We'll have it early. Aunty Nellie will be expecting us."

The three families gathered at Lonsdale Road as if by prior arrangement, only Raymond was absent. As a member of the Territorials he had already been called up. All conversation related to the war and its implications. After a while, Aunty Nellie with her usual optimism butted in. "Mr. Milner says it'll be over by Christmas." We were only too happy to accept Mr. Milner's uncorroborated statement. But Uncle Arnold unscrewed his cigarette from his lips and said drily, "H'mph, that's a surprising bit of quick thinking on Mr. Milner's part, when you remember Nellie it took him two hours to organise your rescue when the bedroom window sash cord broke, and trapped you by the legs. You have to admit a war could've been fought and won in the time." This fond memory produced a muted burst of laughter. The truth was, we wanted to believe Mr. Milner's confidence in a short conflict.

That first day of the Second World War Aunty Lizzie distinguished herself by having the final word, which is perhaps as it should be. Adjusting her unbecoming glasses, she burrowed into the depths of her handbag in a triumphant foray for her Bismuth tablets. She popped one in her mouth, snapped her handbag shut and eyeing my mother and Aunty Nellie with the supremacy permitted to the eldest, shifted the Bismuth tablet to her cheek and said half jokingly, "Now there's a war on we shall be known as Lizbeth, Margaret and Ellen."

So my mother had been right. Things could never be the same again. How could they be if Lizzie, Maggie and Nellie disappeared for ever? And they did. This first, small contribution to change was adopted with pleasure. With the acquisition of posher names, my mother and her sisters found new confidence. They faced the unknowable future with renewed enthusiasm. Everything was bound to be all right for, through all the trials and tribulations which would lead us to those undiscovered ends they held firmly to their belief that:

There's nothing worth the wear of winning,
But laughter and the love of friends.